YOUR FUTURE

Rights,
relationships
and
responsibilities

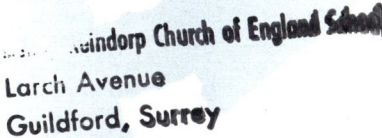

Collins

John Foster
Diane Craven

Published by HarperCollins*Publishers* Limited
77–85 Fulham Palace Road
Hammersmith
London W6 8JB

www.**Collins**Education.com
On-line support for school and colleges

First published 2001
Reprinted 2001 (twice)
ISBN 0 00 327360 1

John Foster and Diane Craven assert the moral right to be identified as authors of this work.

British Library Catalogue in Publication Data
A catalogue record for this publication is available from the British Library.

Commissioned by Thomas Allain-Chapman
Project management by Gaynor Spry
Edited by Kim Richardson
Picture research by Suzanne Williams
Design and layout by Ken Vail Graphic Design, Cambridge
Cover design by Ken Vail Graphic design, Cambridge
Cover photograph BRITSTOCK-IFA
Production by Katie Morris
Printed and bound by Scotprint

Photographs

The publishers would like to thank the following for permission to reproduce photographs (the page number is followed, where necessary, by t-top, b-bottom, l-left, r-right, c-centre).

Bubbles Photo Library: 8c/Lucy Tizard, 8b/John Powell, 10t (Ian West), 11/Frans Rombout, 21/Chris Rout, 23b/Dr Hercules Robinson, 34/Frans Rombout, 41tr/Jennie Woodcock, 41bl & 42/Denise Hager, 43/Frans Rombout, 44/John Powell, 47 & 48/Angela Hampton, 55t/Denise Hager, 63tr/Jennie Woodcock, 63cl & 68/Pauline Cutler, 80/Frans Rombout, 81t/John Powell, 83tr/Frans Rombout, 85/Jennie Woodcock, 87/Pauline Cutler; GettyOne Stone: 6/Naile Goelbasi, 7/Christian Hoehn, 10c/Laurence Monneret, 10b/Julie Fisher, 12/Girl Ray, 13/Andy Sachs, 14/Ian O'Leary, 15/Laurence Monneret, 16/Graeme Harris, 17/Lonnie Duka, 20/Ian Shaw, 22/Andy Sachs, 23t/Adrian Weinbrecht, 24/Mark Joseph, 25/Myrleen Cate, 26/David Oliver, 29/Tim Brown, 30/Ancil Nance, 40/Brian Bailey, 41tl/Robert C Benson, 46/Peter Cade, 52/Tony Hutchings, 51/Ranald Mackechnie, 56/Philip Lee Harvey, 57/Garry Wade, 58/Anthony Marsland, 59/Angela Wyant, 62/Steve Taylor, 64/Seth Kushner, 66/Timothy Shonnard, 67/Philip Lee Harvey, 69/Nick Daly, 70/Jerome Tisne, 71/Jon Riley, 72/Ian O'Leary, 73/Howard Kingsnorth, 74/Bruce Ayres, 76/Dale Durfee, 77/Laurence Monneret, 78/Stewart Cohen, 79/Mark Douet, 81b/Matthias Clamer, 82tl/David Hanover, 82br/Elie Bernager, 83tl/David Yung Wolff, 91/Jonathan Morgan, 95/David Young Wolff; Photofusion: 8t/Mark Campbell, 33/Liam Bailey, 38/Paul Baldesare, 49/Ute Klaphake, 60/Ian Simpson, 61/Paul Doyle, 63br/Martin Wilson, 75/Paul Doyle, 84/Gary Parker, 86/Gina Glover, 92/Liam Bailey; Press Association: 9tl/Anthony Harvey, 9tr/Kipa Press, 9b & 88/European Press Agency, 89/Ben Curtis, 93 & 94/European Press Agency; Rex Features: 36/Steve Wood, 37/Don Iron, 39/Woman's Own, 45/Dennis Stone; Science Photo Library: 53, 54/NIBSC, 55b/Jerry Mason, 65 BSIP/Beranger; John Walmsley: 19, 27

Acknowledgements

The publishers gratefully acknowledge the following for permission to reproduce copyright material. Every effort has been made to trace copyright holders, but in some cases this has proved impossible. The publishers would be happy to hear from any copyright holder that has not been acknowledged.

'The media and teenage values' (p7) adapted from *Media Studies for GCSE* by Peter Wall and Paul Walker, published by HarperCollins publishers. Reprinted with permission of the publishers; 'Brand mania' (p8) from *No Logo* by Naomi Klein, published by Flamingo in 2000; 'Ideals and heroes' (p9) adapted from *Introducing Moral Issues* by Joe Jenkins, published by Heinemann. Reprinted by permission of REPP; 'Be assertive, not aggressive' (p10) adapted from *Confident Children* by Gael Lindenfield, published by Thorsons; 'Understanding assertive, aggressive and passive behaviour' and 'Know your rights' (p10) from *Teen Esteem: A Self-Direction Manual for Young Adults* (2nd edition) © 2000 by Pat Palmer and Melissa Alberti Froehner. Reproduced for John Foster and Diane Craven by permission of Impact Publishers Inc, PO Box 6016, Atascadero, CA 93423. Further reproduction prohibited; 'Fogging' and 'The broken record' (p11) adapted from *Confident Children* by Gael Lindenfield, published by Thorsons; 'From mad to mean' (p12) from *Teen Esteem: A Self-Direction Manual for Young Adults* (2nd edition) © 2000 by Pat Palmer and Melissa Alberti Froehner. Reproduced for John Foster and Diane Craven by permission of Impact Publishers Inc, PO Box 6016, Atascadero, CA 93423. Further reproduction prohibited; 'How do you use your time?' (p14), 'Making a revision calendar' (p16), 'Reviewing your results' (p18) and 'Planning your answers' (p19) adapted from *Studywise 2* by John Foster, published by HarperCollins Publishers; 'The question: a new internet credit card for kids will make it easier for children to spend their pocket money on the web. Is this a good idea?' (p21) from *The Guardian*. © *The Guardian*; 'She owes me money' (p22) from MIZZ © MIZZ/IPC Syndication 1997. Reprinted by permission of IPC Syndication; 'Types of skills' (p25) adapted from *Keep Your Options Open* by Vivienne Neale, published by Hodder and Stoughton in 1997. Reprinted by permission of the publishers; 'What my job is like' (p26), 'Applying for a job' (p27) and 'How to do well at interviews' (p29) adapted from *Job Book 2001. Job Book 2001* is produced by Springboard. Springboard is a free careers and education information service for 16-18s, teachers and their parents. Register for free online at www. spingboard.co.uk; 'Presenting your best side' (p28) adapted from an article by Serena Pym in *Streetwyse*; 'Communicating well' (p29) from *Jobfinder* by Christine Ingham, published by Fourth Estate; 'Thin stars on TV "put pressure on the young"' (p36) adapted from an article by Sandra Barwick in the *Daily Telegraph*, 31 May 2000. © Telegraph Group Limited, 31 May 2000. Reprinted with permission; 'Fashion chief defends use of skinny models', adapted from 'Fashion chief accused over dieting plague' by David Smith and Kirsty Walker, and '60,000 suffer eating disorders' (p36) from *Daily Express*, 31 May 2000. Used with permission; 'We must change our ideal of beauty' (p37) by Dr Phil Hammond, from *Daily Express*, 31 May 2000. Used with permission; 'Crash dieting can damage your health' (p38) from *Eating Disorders* by Kate Haycock, published by Wayland Publishers. Reprinted by permission of Hodder & Stoughton Limited; 'The right amount of the right foods' (p38) from *Eating Disorders* by Jenny Bryan, published by Hodder & Stoughton Limited. Reprinted by permission of Hodder & Stoughton Limited; 'Don't be conned - learn to like the way you are' (p39) from *Am I Normal?* By Anita Naik, published by Hodder & Stoughton Limited. Reprinted by permission of Hodder & Stoughton Limited; 'Why exercise?' (p40) adapted from *Wise Guides: Eating* By Anita Naik, published by Hodder & Stoughton Limited. Reprinted by permission of Hodder & Stoughton Limited; 'Types of exercise' (p41) from *Every Girl's Lifeguide* by Dr Miriam Stoppard, published by Dorling Kindersley Limited. © Dr Miriam Stoppard. Reprinted by permission of Dorling Kindersley and the author. See www.miriamstoppard.com; 'Looking at lifestyles' (p41) from *Health and Fitness in Focus* by Hilary Tuncliffe, first published in the UK by Franklin Watts, a division of The Watts Publishing Group Limited, 96 Leonard Street, London EC2A 4XD. Used with permission; 'What is pre-menstrual syndrome?' (p42) from *Every Girl's Lifeguide* by Dr Miriam Stoppard, published by Dorling Kindersley Limited. © Dr Miriam Stoppard. Reprinted by permission of Dorling Kindersley and the author. See www.miriamstoppard.com; 'How do you know if you've got PMS?' (p42), 'Julia's story' and 'How to beat your period blues' (p43) adapted from *It Happened to Me* by Lesley Johnston, published by Macmillan. Reprinted with permission of the publishers; 'Acne' (p44) from *Every Girl's Lifeguide* by Dr Miriam Stoppard, published by Dorling Kindersley Limited. © Dr Miriam Stoppard. Reprinted by permission of Dorling Kindersley and the author. See www.miriamstoppard.com; 'Acne - your questions answered' (p44) adapted from an article by Peter Moore in *The Guardian*, 30 August 1994. © The Guardian, 30 August 1994. Used with permission; 'Acne made me feel miserable' (p44) adapted from 'Acne made my life hell' by Simone Cave in MIZZ. © Simone Cave/MIZZ/IPC Syndication. Used with permission of IPC Syndication; 'Stay safe in the sun' (p45) from *Every Girl's Lifeguide* by Dr Miriam Stoppard, published by Dorling Kindersley Limited. © Dr Miriam Stoppard. Reprinted by permission of Dorling Kindersley and the author. See www.miriamstoppard.com; 'Stressed out!!!!' (p46), 'Seven ways of beating stress' and 'League table of what stresses you out' (p47) by Victoria Stanley, from *Daily Telegraph*'s T2 section, 25 September 2000. © Telegraph Group Limited, 25 September 2000. Used with permission; 'The signs of stress' (p46) from *Health and Fitness in Focus* by Hilary Tuncliffe, first published in the UK by Franklin Watts, a division of The Watts Publishing Group Limited, 96 Leonard Street, London EC2A 4XD. Used with permission; 'What depression is' (p48) from *Understanding Depression* © 2000 Mind. Reprinted by permission of Mind (National Association for Mental Health); 'What causes depression?' and 'How do I know if I have serious depression?' (p48)' from *Bad Hair Day* by Nancy Scott-Cameron, published by Element Books; 'What does it feel like to be severely depressed?' (p48) from *It Happened to Me* by Lesley Johnston, published by Macmillan. Reprinted with permission of the publishers; 'I want to kill myself' (p49) from *Am I Normal?* By Anita Naik, published by Hodder & Stoughton Limited. Reprinted by permission of Hodder & Stoughton Limited; 'Saying no to sex?' (p51) from *Life Files: Sex Matters* by Julian Cohen, published by Evans Brothers Limited, 2a Portman Mansions, London W1U 6UR. Copyright © Evans Brothers Limited 1997. All rights reserved. Used with permission; 'Teenagers regret having sex too early' (p51) from *Young People's Sexual Attitudes and Behaviour* by C. Ray, Sex Education Forum, Highlight Series No 158, National Children's Bureau. Reprinted by permission; 'Contraception' (p52) adapted from *Life Files: Sex Matters* by Julian Cohen, published by Evans Brothers Limited, 2a Portman Mansions, London W1U 6UR. Copyright © Evans Brothers Limited 1997. All rights reserved. Used with permission; 'Sexually transmitted infections' (p53) from *Sexually Transmitted Infections* produced by Health Education Authority in 1998. Reprinted by permission of Health Promotion England; 'HIV, AIDS and sex' (p54) adapted from *HIV and AIDS Information for Young People* produced by AVERT. Reprinted with permission; 'I took a risk and paid the price' (p55) from *A One Night Stand Almost Ruined my Life* © MIZZ/IPC Syndication. Reprinted by permission of IPC Syndication; 'Having a HIV test' (p55) adapted from *Life Files: Sex Matters* by Julian Cohen, published by Evans Brothers Limited, 2a Portman Mansions, London W1U 6UR. Copyright © Evans Brothers Limited 1997. All rights reserved. Used with permission; graph (p56) from *The Guardian*, 10 October 1999. © The Guardian, 10 October 1999. Used with permission; 'Alcohol - what are its effects?' (p56) adapted from an article in the T2 section of the *Daily Telegraph*, 5 July 2000. © Telegraph Group Limited, 5 July 2000. Used with permission; and 'The hard facts' (p56), 'If alcohol disappeared, there'd be no way to enjoy yourself' and 'Reasons for not getting completely trashed' (p57) adapted from *Alcohol: Facts for Young People* produced by the Health Education Authority. Reprinted by permission of Health Promotion England; 'So why do people do it?' (p57) and ' Have you got a problem?' (p58) from *Wise Guides: Drugs* by Anita Naik, published by Hodder & Stoughton Limited. Reprinted by permission of Hodder & Stoughton Limited; 'Drugs factfile' (p60) from *Right Angle* no. 30, summer 2000, produced by Save the Children. Used with permission; 'All drugs carry risks' (p60) from *The Score: Facts about Drugs* produced by the Health Education Authority. Reprinted by permission of Health Promotion England; 'Why do young people use drugs?' (p60) and 'Time for a change in the law?' (p62) from *Life File: Drugs* by Julian Cohen, published by Evans Brothers Limited, 2a Portman Mansions, London W1U 6UR. Copyright © Evans Brothers Limited 1995. All rights reserved. Used with permission; 'What about the law?' (p61) from *A Parent's Guide to Drugs and Solvents* produced by the Health Education Authority. Reprinted by permission of Health Promotion England; 'Cannabis factfile' (p62) adapted from *Wise Guides: Drugs* by Anita Naik, published by Hodder & Stoughton Limited. Reprinted by permission of Hodder & Stoughton Limited; 'Bishop: teach young people how to use cannabis' (p62) by Jack Sullivan in *The Independent*, 17 August 1999. © The Independent, 17 August 1999. Used with permission of The Independent Syndication; 'Schools and drugs - what do you think?' (p63) from *Drugs in Schools* by Jennifer Amory in the T2 section of the *Daily Telegraph*. © Telegraph Group. Used with permission; 'The addict's story - paying for his habit' (p64) from *Check It!* produced by Metropolitan Police Service. Used with permission; 'Heroin factfile' (p65) adapted from *The Score: Facts about Drugs* produced by Health Education Authority. Reprinted by permission of Health Education England; 'Heroin users getting younger' (p65) from 'Abusers start at 15' by Alan Travis in *The Guardian*, 15 April 2000. © The Guardian, 15 April 2000. Used with permission; 'Being in love' (p66), 'Be yourself' (p67) and 'What makes a relationship work?' (p68) from *Relationships* by Pete Sanders and Steve Myers, first published in the UK by Franklin Watts in 1994, a division of The Watts Publishing Group Limited, 96 Leonard Street, London EC2A 4XD. Used with permission; 'What boys look for' and 'What girls look for' (p66) from *Every Girl's Lifeguide* by Dr Miriam Stoppard, published by Dorling Kindersley Limited. © Dr Miriam Stoppard. Reprinted by permission of Dorling Kindersley and the author. See www.miriamstoppard.com; 'What to do if your boyfriend is jealous' (p68) from *Friends or Enemies?* by Anita Naik, published by Hodder & Stoughton Limited. Reprinted by permission of Hodder & Stoughton Limited; 'Breaking up' (p69) from *Love Lines* by Caroline Plaisted, published by Element Books; 'Your growing independence' (p72) from *Every Girl's Lifeguide* by Dr Miriam Stoppard, published by Dorling Kindersley Limited. © Dr Miriam Stoppard. Reprinted by permission of Dorling Kindersley and the author. See www.miriamstoppard.com; 'Family arguments' (p72) from *Families: can't live with them, can't live without them* by Anita Naik, published by Hodder & Stoughton Limited. Reprinted by permission of Hodder & Stoughton Limited; 'Your needs, rights and privileges' and 'Your own space' (p73) from *Every Girl's Lifeguide* by Dr Miriam Stoppard, published by Dorling Kindersley Limited. © Dr Miriam Stoppard. Reprinted by permission of Dorling Kindersley and the author. See www.miriamstoppard.com;
'Robina's story' (p74) from 'Smile' by Ruby Khan. Extract from *Family Fall Out - young women talk about family break up* edited by Helen Hines, published in great Britain by The Women's Press Limited, 1999, 34 Great Sutton Street, London EC1V 0LQ. Used by permission of The Women's Press; 'For the child's sake' (p75) by Adrienne Katz from *The Guardian*, 16 August 2000. © Adrienne Katz, 16 August 2000. Used with permission; 'The death of a parent' (p76) from *Every Girl's Lifeguide* by Dr Miriam Stoppard, published by Dorling Kindersley Limited. © Dr Miriam Stoppard. Reprinted by permission of Dorling Kindersley and the author. See www.miriamstoppard.com; 'The death of a friend' (p77) from 'How to cope when someone you love dies' from *Shout* issue 96. © D. C. Thomson & Co Ltd. Used with permission; 'Helping a bereaved friend' and 'Suicide' (p77) from *Families: can't live with them, can't live without them* by Anita Naik published by Hodder & Stoughton Limited. Reprinted by permission of Hodder & Stoughton Limited; 'Cohabitation - a fragile short-lived state' and 'Why cohabit?' (p79) from *Marriage Lite* by Patricia Morgan, published by CIVITAS. Used with permission; 'Together apart' (p79) from *The Guardian*, 4 September 2000. © The Guardian, 4 September 2000. Used with permission; 'Arranged marriages' (p80) from *Speaking Out: Black Girls in Britain* by Audrey Osler, published by Virago 1989. Reprinted by kind permission of the author; 'No regrets' (p80) from 'Till death do us part' by Caitlyn McCarthy in *More!*, 20 September-3 October 2000. Reprinted by permission of EMAP Elan Syndication; 'Can your first love last forever?' (p81) by Busola Odulate and Sally Brook in *The Sunday People*, 30 July 2000. Reprinted by permission of the Mirror Group; 'Why do so many teenage marriages fail?' (p81) adapted from an article in *Mizz*. © MIZZ/IPC Syndication. Reprinted by permission of IPC Syndication; 'Your baby's needs' (p82) and 'What do children need?' (p83) adapted from *Putting Children First* and *Listening to Children* produced by the NSPCC. Used with permission; 'Most parents in favour of smacking children' (p83) by Peter Foster, in *Daily Telegraph*, 2 August 2000. © Telegraph Group Limited, 2 August 2000. Used with permission; 'Being a teenage mother' (p84) adapted from 'I had twins at 13' by Annette Morgan, from *Sugar*, September 2000. Reprinted by permission of Attic Futura; 'Boys to pay for teen pregnancy' (p84) by David Brindle in *The Guardian*, 14 June 1999 © The Guardian, 14 June 1999. Used with permission; 'Hurdles for the teenage father' (p85) from 'Teenage fathers' by Maureen Freely, in *The Guardian*, 8 September 1999. © The Guardian, 8 September 1999. Used with permission; 'Marriage before fatherhood' (p85) by Catherine Elsworth in *The Sunday Telegraph*, 9 April 2000. © Telegraph Group Limited, 9 April 2000. Used with permission; 'GPs back reform of abortion law' (p86) by Sarah Boseley in *The Guardian*, 23 June 1999. © The Guardian, 23 June 1999. Used with permission; 'The only choice for me' and 'Abortion factfile' (p87) from 'Abortion' by Kate Aston in *19* © 19/IPC Syndication. Reprinted with permission of IPC Syndication; quote (p87) from *Teenage Pregnancy*, a report by the Social Exclusion Unit. Used with permission; 'Scientists create first genetically modified monkey' (p88) by Roger Highfield in the *Daily Telegraph*, 12 January 2001. © Telegraph Group Limited, 12 January 2001. Used with permission; 'GM foods - do the benefits outweigh the risks?' (p89) from *Whats the Big Idea? Genetics* by Martin Brookes published by Hodder & Stoughton Limited. Reprinted by permission of Hodder & Stoughton Limited; 'Is GM food dangerous?' (p89) from 'Genetic modifications - questions and answers' by George Jones in *Daily Telegraph*, 15 February 1999. © Telegraph Group Limited, 15 February 1999. Used with permission; 'GM food gets clean bill of health' (p89) by Charles Glover in *Daily Telegraph*, 2 March 2000. © Telegraph Group Limited, 2 March 2000. Used with permission; 'Euthanasia - for and against' (p90) from factsheets produced by the Voluntary Euthanasia Society. Used with permission; 'Dutch carry "declaration of life" cards' (p90) from 'Dutch carry card that says - don't kill me doctor' by Rachel Bridge in *Daily Telegraph*, 18 October 1998. © Telegraph Group Limited, 18 October 1998. Used with permission; 'Living wills – for and against' (p91) from *Living Wills* produced by the Voluntary Euthanasia Society, used with permission, and from 'Claire Rayner debates the pros and cons of living wills', an article in *The Sunday Times* © Claire Rayner. Reprinted by permission of Clairemond Limited; 'Racial harassment' and 'Standing up against racism' (p92) from *Racism* by Jagdish Gundara and Roger Hewitt published by Evans Brothers Limited, 2a Portman Mansions, London W1U 6UR. Copyright © Evans Brothers Limited. All rights reserved. Used with permission; 'Sexual harassment' (p93) from *Life Files: Sex Matters* by Julian Cohen, published by Evans Brothers Limited, 2a Portman Mansions, London W1U 6UR. Copyright © Evans Brothers Limited 1997. All rights reserved. Used with permission; 'Should offensive pop songs be censored?' (p93) adapted from 'Eminem - should he be censored?' by Jerome Monahan in *The Guardian*, 9 January 2001. © Jerome Monahan, 9 January 2001. Used with permission; 'Grandmother has her day in court' (p94) by Kirsty Scott, in *The Guardian*, 8 August 2000. © The Guardian, 8 August 2000. Used with permission; 'Animal rights gang sends victim a nail-bomb' (p94) by Philip Johnston in *Daily Telegraph*, 12 January 2001. © Telegraph Group Limited, 12 January 2001. Used with permission; 'Miracle work on deprived estate' (p95) by Helen Carter in *The Guardian*, 8 August 2000. © The Guardian, 8 August 2000. Used with permission.

Contents

Introduction 5

1 Developing Your Image and Lifestyle 6

2 Managing Your Emotions 10

3 How to Study 14

4 Managing Your Money 20

5 Thinking About Careers 24

6 Choosing Your Future: Options at 16+ 30

7 Recording Your Achievements 34

8 Eating and Exercise 36

9 Health Matters 42

10 Dealing with Stress and Depression 46

11 Safer Sex 50

12 Teenage Drinking 56

13 Drugs Issues 60

14 Friends and Relationships 66

15 Family Matters 72

16 Marriage and Partnerships 78

17 Becoming a Parent 82

18 Social and Moral Dilemmas: Where Do You Stand? 86

19 Standing up for Your Beliefs 92

Index 96

Personal, Social and Health Education · Your Future

Developing Self-awareness	Keeping Healthy	Relationships and Responsibilities
Developing your image and lifestyle	Eating and exercise	Friends and relationships
Managing your emotions	Health matters	Family matters
How to study	Dealing with stress and depression	Marriage and partnerships
Managing your money	Safer sex	Becoming a parent
Thinking about careers	Teenage drinking	Social and moral dilemmas: where do you stand?
Choosing your future: options at 16+	Drugs issues	Standing up for your beliefs
Recording your achievements		

Introduction

To the student

Your Future provides a comprehensive course in Personal, Social and Health Education at Key Stage 4 (S3, S4). There are nineteen units divided into three broad groups, focusing on self-awareness, developing a healthy lifestyle and developing relationships and understanding responsibilities.

Developing self-awareness

The seven self-awareness units in *Your Future* concentrate on developing your self-knowledge and your ability to manage your emotions, how to organise your study-time and make decisions about your career paths and how to manage your money.

The opening unit, 'Developing your image and lifestyle', contains activities to help you think about your own identity and personality and to reflect on what influences your behaviour, what your values and beliefs are, the people you admire and what image you want to convey of yourself. 'Managing your emotions' aims to develop your assertiveness skills, explaining the difference between assertive, aggressive and passive styles of behaviour and how to make requests and handle criticism assertively, and gives detailed advice on how to deal with anger, stressing the importance of controlling it, channelling it and using it constructively. 'How to study' is a study-skills unit, focusing on the development of time management skills, on strategies that can be used to plan effective revision and on preparing for examinations. 'Managing your money' explores attitudes to money and some of the problems teenagers have with money and explains how to plan a budget. It also examines all the costs of living in a place of your own.

The other three units in this section are designed to help you make a choice about the path each of you intends to take at 16+. 'Thinking about careers' includes self-assessment activities to enable you to identify your personal strengths and skills, and explains what information you need to find out when investigating and making a decision about a particular career. It also offers guidance on how to apply for a job, how to draft a CV and how to prepare for interviews. 'Choosing your future: options at 16+' explains the pathways that are open to teenagers at 16+ and gives detailed information about the various educational courses that are available. 'Recording your achievements' is a self-assessment unit, explaining how to prepare and write a personal statement to put in your file.

Keeping healthy

These six units are designed to complement the work on health education taking place elsewhere in the curriculum. 'Eating and exercise' explores the pressure that the media puts on young people to be slim and how this is a factor contributing to eating disorders, examines the diet culture and how dieting can damage your health, and explains the importance of exercise and the value of different types of exercise. 'Health matters' explains what Pre-Menstrual Syndrome is and how to cope with it and looks at skin care, focusing on the causes and treatment of acne, how to stay safe in the sun and the fashions for tattooing and body piercing. 'Dealing with stress and depresssion'

focuses on teenage stress and how to cope with it, explains what depression is, how to recognise if you are severely depressed and what to do in order to deal with severe depression. 'Safer sex' focuses on the importance of communication as crucial to mature and responsible sexual activity, examines the pressures on teenagers to have sex and presents information on methods of contraception, STDs, HIV and AIDS and how to protect yourself against infection. 'Teenage drinking' presents facts about alcohol and its effects, explores the reasons why teenagers drink, defines problem drinking and looks at the consequences of excessive drinking. 'Drugs issues' focuses on why young people use drugs, explains the laws on drugs, examines the arguments for and against changing the law on cannabis, considers how schools should deal with drug incidents and presents information about heroin and a case study of a drug addict.

Relationships and responsibilities

The six units in this section of the course not only cover key areas within the Personal, Social and Health education curriculum, but also important features of the citizenship curriculum, dealing with relationships within society, and the responsibilities that individuals have both within their families and within the community.

The 'Friends and relationships' unit focuses on close relationships, exploring what love means and what boys and girls look for in members of the opposite sex, what makes relationships flourish and how to manage the break-up of a relationship. There is also a section on same-sex relationships and on attitudes towards homosexuality. 'Family matters' examines the needs and rights of teenagers, exploring how growing independence and increasing responsibilities are linked. There are also sections on coping with divorce and separation and coping with bereavement. 'Marriage and partnerships' focuses on the reasons for marrying and looks at why a growing number of couples choose to live together rather than marry. The custom of arranged marriages is explored and there is a discussion of the reasons behind the failure of so many teenage marriages. 'Becoming a parent' examines what parenthood entails, what young children need and what it is like being a parent while you are still a teenager. 'Social and moral dilemmas' presents information for discussion on three controversial issues – abortion, genetic engineering and euthanasia. The final unit, 'Standing up for your beliefs', emphasises the importance of speaking out against racism and sexism. It also includes case histories of people who have been prepared to take action as a matter of principle in order to draw attention to policies which they believe to be wrong and to improve the environment in which they live.

The various activities provide you with opportunities to explore your own character, to examine your feelings, to consider your opinions and thus to develop your self-awareness, and learn how to take responsibility for managing your studies and planning your future. The group discussion activities involve you in learning how to co-operate and negotiate. You are presented with situations in which you have to work with others, to analyse information, to consider moral and social dilemmas and to make choices and decisions. There are also opportunities for learning through role play, for example enabling you to understand the consequences of acting in an aggressive, passive or assertive way.

Developing Your Image and Lifestyle

Who am I? Developing a sense of your own identity

Your personal history

Each of us has a personal history which contributes to our identity. Thinking about our own background can help us to develop our sense of identity.

Here's what Rajid Singh wrote about himself after thinking about his background:

I'm a fifteen-year-old boy whose grandfather came to England from India in the 1950s, so some people would call me a third generation British boy of Indian descent. But I just think of myself as a British boy who lives in Leicester.

We are a Sikh family and our religion is very important to us. So I always try to behave as a Sikh is expected to behave and to follow the traditional Sikh teachings.

We've still got family connections in India and it's my ambition to go there one day – though I expect the people there would find me very British!

In pairs

With a friend, discuss the following questions. Then each write a statement about yourself, similar to Rajid's statement, saying who you are and describing your family background.

1. What do you know about your family history – about your mother and her family and/or your father and his family?

2. People sometimes think of themselves as belonging to a particular class, either because of their family's economic circumstances or because of the jobs their parents did. Does your family think of itself as belonging to a particular class?

3. What is your nationality? Do any of your family feel strong ties with another country because they were born or brought up there?

4. What language do you speak at home? Do you speak a dialect? Do you speak with an accent? (A dialect is a language variety which has some distinctive words and grammar. Accent refers to the way words are pronounced.)

5. What is your family's religion? Does religion play an important part in your life?

6. Have you always lived in the same area? Do you feel you belong to one particular place more than any other?

Your personality

Each of us has our own personality. Thinking about the features of your character can help you to understand what sort of person you are and further develop your sense of identity.

Psychologists sometimes describe people as being either **introverts** or **extroverts**. An introvert is someone who tends to look inwards towards themselves, while an extrovert is someone who looks outwards towards other people. No one is ever a complete introvert or a complete extrovert. But, depending on our personality, each of us tends to be either more of an introvert or more of an extrovert.

In pairs

Work with a friend. Study the table below and decide **a)** whether you think you are more of an introvert or more of an extrovert, and **b)** whether your friend is more of an introvert than an extrovert. Then discuss what you decided and say why.

Introverts

Quiet and thoughtful.

Keep themselves to themselves and are happy to spend time on their own.

May act shyly and take their time before mixing at parties.

Tend to form a few close friendships and keep them a long time.

Find it hard to push themselves forward.

Think carefully before volunteering.

Often control their anger rather than express it outwardly.

May prefer to have a career where they work on their own.

Extroverts

Lively and boisterous.

Enjoy being in a crowd.

Outgoing, tend to be the life and soul of parties.

Make friends easily, but may drop them just as fast.

Push themselves forward and are prepared to make a fool of themselves.

Always willing to have a go, sometimes without thinking.

Express their anger when they feel it.

Often prefer careers in which they come into contact with lots of people.

What influences your behaviour?

How you behave depends not only on your personality, but on how you are influenced by other people. The main influence on you is likely to be your parents or guardian and any other adults with whom you live or are in regular contact, such as grandparents or other family relatives. Then there's the influence of the people whom you choose as your close friends.

You are also influenced by the communities to which you belong – the school you go to and any religious community of which you are a member. There's the wider community too – the country in which you live, its culture and its laws. Finally, there's the influence of the media – the TV programmes you watch, the adverts you see, the books, newspapers and magazines you read and the music you listen to.

friends and acquaintances
my country, its culture and laws
magazines
television
newspapers
grandparents
advertising
religion
parent(s) or carer(s)
my school
brothers and sisters
teachers
pop music
books
my local community
close friends

In pairs

On your own, study the diagram (above, right) and decide how much you think your behaviour is conditioned by each of the different influences. Rank them on a scale of 1–5 (1 = a very great influence, 5 = hardly an influence at all). Then share your views with a partner.

Your values and beliefs

Another important aspect of your identity concerns your values and beliefs. Where you stand on moral issues will help you to decide how you want to live your life and what sort of people you want to have as your friends.

In groups

For each statement below decide on your own whether you agree, disagree or feel it depends on the circumstances. Then form groups and discuss your views.

1. Sex before marriage is wrong.
2. It's acceptable to lie about your qualifications in a job interview.
3. Swearing is offensive.
4. People who sell drugs are evil.
5. Fighting is a good way of settling an argument.
6. Smacking children should not be allowed.
7. You should always be willing to cover up for a friend.
8. It's OK to go out with two people at the same time.
9. You should tell someone if they undercharge you.
10. You shouldn't give money to beggars.
11. You should never break a promise.
12. Parents should be able to choose the sex of their babies.

" The main influences on young people today are the media, in particular television and the internet. In the past, the family was a far more important influence than it is today. But nowadays the family is often fragmented and scattered. It can be difficult for parents who want to do so to pass on their own values and beliefs to their children when they have to compete with what young people are seeing and hearing on TV and discovering on the internet. "

The media and teenage values

Many people blame the media for the irresponsible behaviour of some teenagers. There are many violent and sexual images in the media, which they say lead to more violence and sexual activity in society.

They have claimed that the portrayal of sex on TV has led to a drop in what are called moral standards. They say that young people have copied characters in television dramas and become involved in sexual activity without considering its consequences.

Newspapers and magazines have not escaped criticism. Explicit photography and the detailed descriptions of sex and violence in newspapers have been said to have a negative influence on readers. Magazines aimed at teenagers have been attacked for promoting sexual promiscuity by publishing material on contraception and physical relationships. Music and fashion magazines have been slated for their 'glorification' of the bad behaviour of pop stars. The National Lottery has been accused of encouraging people to gamble by leading them to believe that money and happiness are the same thing.

Adapted from *Media Studies for GCSE* by Peter Wall and Paul Walker

In groups

1. Discuss the view about the main influences on young people (above) and say why you agree or disagree with it.
2. Discuss the passage 'The media and teenage values'. How important is the media in constructing your own sense of values?

You and your appearance

It is often said that you shouldn't judge a person by their appearance. But the first impression you get of a person is from the way they dress and the way they look. Your appearance makes a statement about you to other people.

Your clothes

Clothes mark out rich from poor, ruler from ruled, women from men. They show the kind of work people do – a farmer wears different clothes from a banker or a dancer. Clothes vary from country to country and culture to culture. They can also vary according to fashion.

Everyone in the UK today is affected by fashion. Fashion means rapidly changing styles: it means competition to keep up with the latest 'look'. These styles are dictated to us by a multi-million pound industry, which depends on a world-wide chain of labour and materials often supplied by people in developing countries.

But we don't just wear clothes to be fashionable. Dress is an outward sign of our inner character. We judge people by what they are wearing, and we know that they judge us in the same way. We might even decide whether they are worth getting to know.

 In groups

1. Discuss the comments of Lisa, Charmain and Damian and Tony. Talk about what different people might want to say about themselves through the way they look.

2. Discuss your own attitudes to clothes and why you dress the way you do.

> We dress like this to be noticed. It's a rebellion against being acceptable.

Damian and Tony

> I've noticed that the clothes I wear in the evening when I'm likely to be meeting boys tend to be the ones I feel sure I look good in. A boy recently accused me and my group of friends of being obsessed with the way we look. I challenged him and said, 'But you do judge girls by their looks, don't you?' and he had to admit I was right.

Charmain

> 'I'm not completely sure, though, why I go on putting a lot of energy into my appearance. Some of my friends think it's a waste of time getting dressed up to go to school, but I want girls as well as boys to think I'm attractive, and I think this is connected with a desire to feel accepted and successful.

Lisa

Changing fashions

 **In groups**

'As a teenager there's a lot of pressure on you to appear cool. That means wearing the right brands. It's ridiculous really, but that's the way it is.' Jason

'The fashion industry is a great big con. No sooner have they finished persuading you to buy one style than they introduce another and try to get you to buy that. We waste too much time thinking about clothes and fashion when there are far more important issues that we ought to be thinking about.' Isla

Discuss these views. How much attention do you pay to fashion? Are you influenced by it a lot? Quite a lot? Not much? Do you think people in general pay too much attention to changes in fashion?

Brand mania

With this wave of brand mania has come a new breed of businessman, one who will proudly inform you that Brand X is not a product but a way of life, an attitude, a set of values, a look, an idea. And it sounds really great – way better than that Brand X is a screwdriver, or a hamburger chain, or a pair of jeans, or even a very successful line of running shoes. Nike, Phil Knight announced in the late eighties, is 'a sports company'; its mission is not to sell shoes but to 'enhance people's lives through sports and fitness' and to 'keep the magic of sports alive' … at Diesel jeans, owner Renzo Rosso told *Paper* magazine, 'We don't sell a product, we sell a style of life. I think we have created a movement … The Diesel concept is everything. It's the way to live, it's the way to wear, it's the way to do something.'

From *No Logo* by Naomi Klein

 **In groups**

1. Read the article 'Brand mania'. Are companies like Nike promoting a particular lifestyle for your benefit or for their profit?

2. Are you a brand maniac? What are the values behind the brands that you buy?

Feedback

Share your views about clothes, fashion and how important your appearance is to you in a class discussion.

Images and ideals

The image that you want to give of yourself may be influenced by the vision you have of the ideal person. So it's worth considering who you look up to and why.

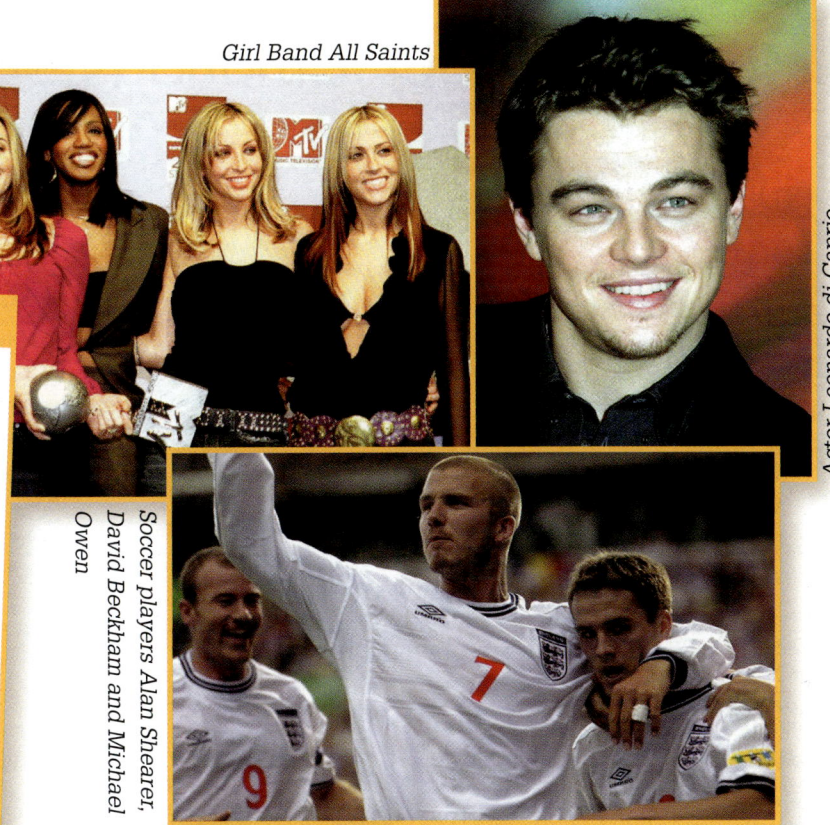

Girl Band All Saints

Soccer players Alan Shearer, David Beckham and Michael Owen

Actor Leonardo di Caprio

Ideals and heroes

When we see a 'hero' in a film, they often show qualities such as bravery, forgiveness and loving kindness. Now, although we might not be able to live in such a way ourselves, we all wish that we could be a little braver, a little wiser, a little more clever, a little more forgiving, a little less jealous, a little less mean, a little less bad-tempered …

We've all got heroes. These days many of our ideal people come from TV, films, magazines or pop music. It is difficult to imagine it, but probably many of the people who are your heroes today might not still be when you're, say, 25. In fact one day when you have children they will probably never have heard of some of today's heroes.

It could be said that there are three types of heroes:

1. Fashionable heroes who are forgotten soon after their moment of fame.

2. Heroes whose names die soon after they do.

3. Heroes whose names live on.

Adapted from *Introducing Moral Issues* by Joe Jenkins

In pairs

1. Write down the names of four people who you consider to be your heroes.

2. Ask your partner to give them a mark (1, 2 or 3) to fit in with the three types of heroes.

3. How many points have your heroes been given?

4. Discuss your heroes and your marks with your partner.

5. Now write down the reasons why you chose those people to be your heroes.

6. Look at the following list of qualities. Mark your heroes according to this list.
   - Good looks
   - Good voice
   - Good dancer or sportsperson
   - Clever
   - Peace loving
   - Wise
   - Works for others
   - Kind and gentle
   - Courageous
   - Sacrificed their lives for others

A cult of celebrity

"We live in an age when there's a cult of celebrity. Many of the people we idolise deserve our admiration for their talents and the use they've made of that talent. But it's absurd to put them up on a pedestal in the way that the media often does. Many celebrities are arrogant and materialistic and some of them are self-indulgent, spending their money on drink and drugs. They certainly aren't the kind of people we should have as role models.

There are plenty of ordinary people who are much more worthy of our respect such as people who work in the community dedicating their lives to helping other people, or people who have overcome severe hardships or disabilities and gone on to lead fulfilling lives. Sometimes I think we've got our priorities all wrong."

Louisa Fairbanks

In groups

Discuss Louisa Fairbanks' views about celebrities and say whether or not you agree with them.

Feedback

Share your views on heroes and celebrities in a class discussion.

for your folder

What would you like people to admire you for? Would it be for doing something courageous? For doing something to help other people? For making full use of your talents? Write a statement saying what you would like to do in your life that would make people regard you with respect.

How to be assertive

Be **assertive**, not **aggressive**

Learning how to be assertive helps us to be ourselves, to respect our own human rights and also to go directly, and energetically, for what we really want without trampling on the needs and rights of others.

Although the word 'assertive' has in the last few years become very freely used, it is still frequently confused with styles of behaviour that are more aggressive, or even passive. While all three basic styles have their uses and misuses, it is the assertive one that is most often used by confident people.

Aggressive, passive and assertive styles

Aggressive

Basic attitude: 'The world is a tough place, but I am the most important person in it and I am prepared to hurt anyone or anything that gets in the way of my happiness or success.'

Typical behaviour: domineering, selfish, forceful, attacking, insensitive, hurtful, righteous, bombastic, prejudiced, blaming, punitive and mistrustful.

Passive

Basic attitude: 'The world is a scary and difficult place to be in and other people are more important and better than me, so I have to please, or appear to please them.'

Typical behaviour: meek, acquiescent, compliant, submissive, resigned, docile, helpless, self-blaming, self-effacing, long-suffering, manipulative.

Assertive

Basic attitude: 'The world is an OK place and I am just as important as anyone else in it and, like everyone else, I have a right to success and happiness.'

Typical behaviour: self-respecting, fair-minded, honest, direct, expressive, challenging, upright, respectful, trusting, co-operative, persistent, innovative and decisive.

Adapted from *Confident Children* by Gael Lindenfield

Understanding assertive, aggressive and passive behaviour

Assertiveness is taking charge of your life: speaking clearly and honestly, asking for what you want and saying no to what you don't want. It is learning to feel valuable, capable and powerful. In other words it is really caring about yourself. But the assertive person helps others feel good about themselves too, by treating them in loving, caring, kind, thoughtful ways.

Aggressive people are like steamrollers – flattening people in their way. Aggressive people get what they want by pushing people around physically, mentally and emotionally. Aggressiveness can cause you to lose your self confidence and feel bad about yourself. Most people don't like being around someone who's being aggressive. They'd rather totally avoid such a person.

Passive people act like doormats. Passive behaviour is doing nothing, playing it safe, keeping your mouth closed. It is being a doormat: letting others walk on you. Other people make decisions for you, tell you what you want to do and run your life. Passive people often get pushed around, stepped on or forgotten. Other people take advantage of them because they won't stand up for themselves. The passive person has a terrible self image, and little self confidence.

Of course, few of us fit neatly into any category – but if you can start seeing yourself 'steamrollering' or playing 'doormat', you're learning to be honest with yourself – a big step on your way toward assertiveness.

Adapted from *Teen Esteem: A Self-direction Manual for Young Adults* by Dr Pat Palmer and Melissa Alberti Froehner

 In groups

1. Discuss the differences between aggressive, passive and assertive styles of behaviour.
2. Why is it important to learn how to behave assertively?

Know your rights

Knowing your rights helps you make decisions and stand up for yourself – it frees you from other people's put downs and manipulations. Here is a list of ten rights:

I claim the right …

1 to be treated with respect
2 to have my own feelings and express them
3 to have my own opinions and express them
4 to be listened to and taken seriously
5 to decide what is important to me
6 to ask for what I want (others have the right to refuse)
7 to make mistakes, and to learn from them
8 to control my own body
9 to have some privacy or space of my own
10 to take responsibility for my own choices, behaviour, thoughts and feelings.

From *Teen Esteem: A Self-direction Manual for Young Adults* by Dr Pat Palmer and Melissa Alberti Froehner

In groups

1. Discuss the list of rights given above. Do you agree with them?
2. Would you like to add anything to the statements or replace some statements with others?
3. Choose the three that you think are the most important and try to put them in rank order. Give reasons for your choices.
4. How do you think you could put these statements into practice? How do you think your life might change as a result?

How to make requests assertively

Asking for what you want can be difficult, especially if you think the other person is likely to refuse. Learn to make requests assertively.

An assertive request is one that is:

- **direct** and does not beat about the bush
- **concise** and doesn't use lots of unnecessary words
- **polite** and shows respect for the other person's situation or feelings (e.g. *'I can see that you're busy, Dad…'*)
- **positive** and indicates, if only through the tone of voice, that you expect to get what you are asking for (in contrast to *'I know you are going to get cross when I ask you…'*)
- **non-threatening** and doesn't include even a 'veiled' punishment (e.g. *'I'll be upset if you don't…'*)
- **non-manipulative** (in contrast to *'John's mother always…'*).

Use the broken record technique, which can help you persist with your requests without getting aggressive.

The broken record

Technique: Calmly repeat over and over again what you want, without responding to unnecessary arguments or put-downs.

Situation: Jane urgently needs the skirt she lent her sister last week (it is the only thing that fits her properly!). Usually these requests end in blazing rows with neither getting what she wants. Note how effective the 'broken record' can be in such a situation.

Jane: Can I please have back the skirt which you borrowed last week?

Rachel: What do you want it back for? You never wear it.

Jane: Can I have the skirt back, please?

Rachel: You're always wanting my things, what about the leggings you took from my room?

Jane: Can I have the skirt back, please?

Rachel: Why do you always leave things to the last minute? Couldn't you have sorted out what you were going to wear last night?

Jane: Can I have the skirt back, please?

Rachel: Oh, all right, I'll get it – but you're not borrowing anything from me tonight.

From *Confident Children* by Gael Lindenfield

" It's OK to compromise

Being assertive does not mean digging your heels in and always getting your own way. A confident person is someone who is prepared to negotiate and accept a compromise. There will be times when you will not be prepared to shift your position, because you feel there is too much at stake. However, at other times the assertive person will feel able to make concessions, in order to resolve the problem and to prevent the situation escalating into a row. "

Erica Stewart

Dealing with criticism

No one likes being criticised. However, if the criticism is justified, you may be able to learn something from it. Try to stay calm and ask yourself: Are they being fair? Could I have behaved differently?

Even if you feel that the criticism is totally unjustified, try to avoid over-reacting and responding aggressively. One way of dealing with unfair or unwanted criticism, especially when it's not worth getting upset over what they are saying, is to use the technique known as fogging. The article below explains how to use it.

Fogging

How it works

- You respond (repeatedly, if necessary) to your critic by *appearing* to agree, indicating that there could be some truth in what he or she is saying (but inwardly telling yourself that your critic is wrong or that you'll think about it).
- The critic eventually gives up!

The fogging technique in action

(Note that the fogging words are underlined and the confidence-boosting self-talk is in brackets.)

Critic: *'You kids are all the same, you never care about anyone else, you've always got that music blasting the house out.'*

Response: '<u>Perhaps you're right</u>, *the music* <u>may</u> *be a bit loud.'* (She seems in a mood, she's having a go at everyone; I know she doesn't really mean it and I am considerate and the music is the same volume as always.)

Adapted from *Confident Children* by Gael Lindenfield

 Role play

In pairs, try out your responses to the following situations:

1. Your friend is going out with a boy she has liked for ages. She asks if she can borrow your new top/bag. You like your friend but you know that she is a bit careless. You don't want to lend her your belongings.

2. Your best mate asks if he can borrow your CD of your favourite group's latest album. You know that he is prone to losing things.

3. You are revising for your GCSEs. Your sister insists on playing music really loudly in her room. The trouble is, you can hear it all, and it's putting you off your work.

4. Your best friend is behind with her coursework in three subjects. Your best subject is English and your friend has asked you to lend her your coursework so that she can 'read it to get some ideas'. You suspect that she really wants to copy it.

Managing your anger

All of us get angry from time to time – anger is a normal human emotion. However, sometimes anger can build up and get out of control. We can lose our temper; shout abuse; be aggressive or even do things which we would normally consider to be violent.

It can also be unhealthy to show no anger at all – even when anger would be a completely justifiable response. Some people have been brought up never to show feelings of anger, so when their needs are not met or people tread on their feelings they just hold their anger inside. Eventually those 'held-in' feelings can make the person ill or depressed.

It's therefore very important to recognize our feelings of anger. It's also important to manage those feelings so that we can behave appropriately towards other people and so that our feelings do not run away with us.

In pairs

Read Melissa's story (below). Discuss this situation and any advice you would give to Melissa.

Have you ever been in a similar situation? Talk about how you dealt with it.

From Mad to Mean – by Melissa

One of my best friends in junior high and high school was extremely loyal – she put up with my moods, was there when I needed her, and stuck by me no matter what. Still, one day I was so angry with her that I wouldn't talk to her. I made sure that I was extra-nice to everybody else that I saw that day, so she would be sure to know that it was she alone that I was furious with.

Finally, during P.E. at the end of the day, she burst into tears and yelled at me, 'I hate it when you're like this! I'd rather have you just yell at me and get it over with than not talk to me! You're not even giving me a chance to apologize!'

I still can't remember why I was so mad at my friend that day. But I don't think I'll ever forget the look on her face – and how awful I felt for really hurting a true friend. How much better it would have been for both of us if I'd been straight with her and told her how I felt right away!

From *Teen Esteem*

What makes you angry?

66 When someone criticises me unfairly. 99

66 People who deliberately put you down. 99

66 Not being allowed to do something I really want to do. 99

'66 When adults won't listen to your point of view. 99

66 People calling me names and making fun of my appearance. 99

66 When someone lets you down. 99

66 When someone sets you up and makes a fool of you in front of your friends. 99

In pairs

What kinds of behaviour make you angry? Think about situations involving your parents, your brothers and sisters, your friends, your teachers, other adults. Make a list of types of behaviour which cause you to feel angry.

What do you do when you are angry?

Different people do different things when they are angry.

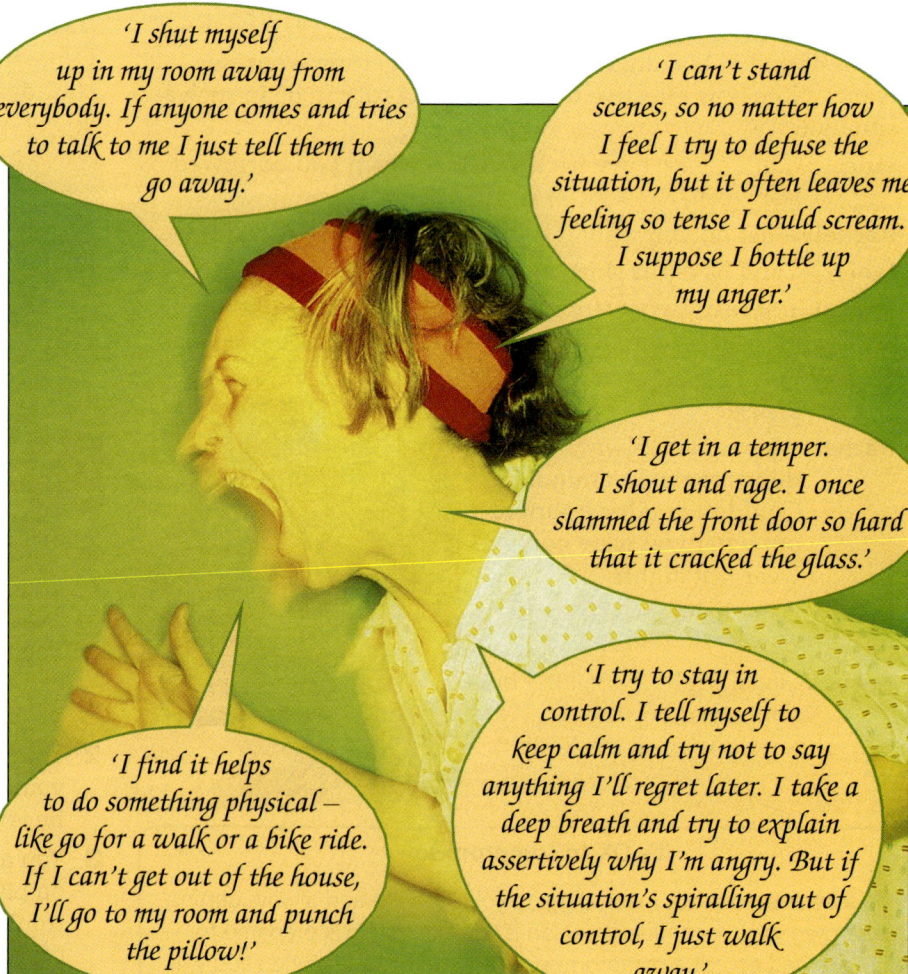

'I shut myself up in my room away from everybody. If anyone comes and tries to talk to me I just tell them to go away.'

'I can't stand scenes, so no matter how I feel I try to defuse the situation, but it often leaves me feeling so tense I could scream. I suppose I bottle up my anger.'

'I get in a temper. I shout and rage. I once slammed the front door so hard that it cracked the glass.'

'I find it helps to do something physical – like go for a walk or a bike ride. If I can't get out of the house, I'll go to my room and punch the pillow!'

'I try to stay in control. I tell myself to keep calm and try not to say anything I'll regret later. I take a deep breath and try to explain assertively why I'm angry. But if the situation's spiralling out of control, I just walk away.'

In groups

Discuss the different things that people do to handle their anger (above). Which are good ways of handling anger? Which are bad ways?

Taking Charge

Say somebody accidentally steps on a homework paper of yours that you worked on for hours. Your teacher is a 'neat freak' and won't be happy about how it looks now. Are you angry? How angry? When you feel your anger starting to build, ask yourself, 'How much does this really matter? Is it worth my getting upset? Will I even care about it two weeks from now? Two days from now? Two hours from now?'

Here are some ways to stop your anger building.

1 **Stop and 'rate' your anger.** Sure, some things are worth getting upset about. If someone steals your bike, you're probably going to be pretty mad (or maybe sad, too). It's a bad thing, right? So, on an 'upset' scale from one to ten, it's about a six or a seven … After all, there are worse things that could happen. Your home could be robbed, and everything you own stolen. That's worse. How would you rate it? An eight? What if a drunk driver killed someone you care about? That's really terrible – probably a ten. So, let's step back for a second … is it really that big a deal that he stepped on your paper? How would you rate it now?

2 You'll save yourself a lot of anger if you learn to step outside yourself and **look at things from the other person's point of view.** We've all had those mornings … You know: you wake up late; can't find the shirt you wanted to wear; somebody ate the last of the good cereal; you forgot your Maths paper was due today, and it's not done; your mum yelled at you … So now you're really late, and you run out the door and right into a neighbour on the pavement … How angry should your neighbour be? Does he know how your morning is going, or does he just think you're some careless kid mowing down everybody who gets in your way? He can choose to get angry, or not to let it upset him. What would you do if you were in his place?

3 **Try to give the other person a break.** Did that lady turn her car right in front of you because she didn't care if she hit you and your bike, or was it because she just found out that a friend is in the hospital and she's just not seeing clearly right now?

4 **Find the humour in the situation.** Once, while driving, Melissa began to get frustrated with the driver of the car in front of her (who seemed to be paying more attention to his frisky dog than to the road): 'So, I joked with my family, "He should let his dog drive — the Chihuahua would probably do a better job!" We laughed at the image of the tiny dog trying to drive the car, and I found my frustration going away.' A good laugh does wonders for a bad mood!

You'll always feel better about yourself if you can make the best of a bad situation – instead of letting it get the best of you.

Adapted from *Teen Esteem* by Pat Palmer and Melissa Alberti Froehner

Finding a Solution

There are times, of course, when you will be angry and need to deal with that anger appropriately. It's not always easy. Here are some helpful guidelines you can use to try to stay in charge of your anger:

◆ Pay attention to what things tend to bother you, and see if you can avoid your angry feelings by being aware of your emotions and working toward a solution. For example, if you always get irritated at the pushing and shoving in the line at the cafeteria, then choose to eat there less often (get up earlier and make your lunch), or talk to school officials to see if the staff can help control the situation. Better yet, work on your own attitude: 'I know I'm going to get bumped around in line, so I'm going to take deep breaths and try to stay relaxed and calm.'

◆ Learn how your body reacts to anger. You can identify what happens with your body as you begin to get angry, and learn how to control your reactions. Think about a time that you were very angry. Picture the scene in your mind, and concentrate on what is happening to your body. Is your heart rate speeding up? Do you feel your face getting hot? Are your teeth clenched? Are your muscles tightening? These are signals that are helpful for you to recognize, so that you can use your 'taking charge' skills to deal with the situation. Learn to relax when you are feeling angry. Now, tighten every muscle in your body that you can – hard! Hold it for a count of ten, and then let every muscle relax. Roll your head on your shoulders and take several deep, slow breaths in and out. Think about a time when you were happy, and let go of your angry feelings.

◆ Express your anger assertively. Of course, there are times when it is appropriate to express your anger, as long as you do it assertively (not aggressively). If you think the situation will be improved by your speaking up, go ahead and do it.

◆ Think about what is causing your anger. It may help you to realize that anger comes from not getting our needs met. When we make sure our own needs are met then we do not need to be angry or depressed. Sometimes just understanding why you are feeling the way you are helps you take charge of how you are feeling.

Adapted from *Teen Esteem* by Pat Palmer and Melissa Alberti Froehner

In pairs

Discuss what you learn from the articles on this page about how to handle anger. What do you think is the most helpful advice? What other ways have you found to deal with anger?

for your folder Write a story about a teenager who fails to control their anger and does something which they regret.

3 How to Study

This unit focuses on three study skills that you need to learn in order to succeed in the subjects that you are studying: how to manage your time, how to plan your revision and how to prepare yourself for exams.

Managing your time

When you start doing GCSE or Standard Grade courses you will need to plan and organize your study time even better than before. If you don't, your work will suffer, and you won't have enough time for leisure activities either.

How do you use your time?

It is worth reviewing your use of time to see if you are using it as efficiently as you could be. One way of doing this is to carry out a daily review. In the evening, just before you go to bed, draw up a chart showing each 15 minute interval throughout the day, and fill in exactly how you spent your time. Then analyse your use of time, trying to identify periods in which you might have used the time more productively. Try to identify time-wasting events, such as:

- time spent chatting at school when you should have been doing private study;
- too much time spent watching TV;
- unnecessarily long telephone calls;
- unproductive time spent waiting or travelling;
- time spent searching the net for no reason;
- time spent searching for books and equipment to enable you to start studying.

Once you have identified any time-wasting events, you need to think of a plan of action that will enable you to eliminate them in the future. For example, you may have to set a time-limit on the length of your telephone calls or to cut down on the amount of TV you allow yourself to watch.

It may also be necessary for you to review your lifestyle completely and to consider whether you have got the right balance between study time and leisure time.

Adapted from Studywise 2

In pairs

Carry out a review of your time, as described in the article above. Show your chart to a partner and discuss these questions:

1. How much study time did you have? Was this enough?
2. How much leisure time did you have? Was this enough?
3. Can you identify any areas where you wasted time?
4. What action could you take to make better use of your time?
5. Do you feel that you need to review your lifestyle more thoroughly in order to focus more on your studies?

Planning ahead: setting goals

As your coursework assignments will sometimes be spread over several weeks it is important to plan ahead so that you don't leave everything to the last minute. Planning will help you break your work down into manageable tasks. It will also motivate you, because each task is a short-term goal which gives you something to aim at, and a sense of achievement when you've completed it.

Draw up a study planner to cover the whole of the next month and mark on it your short-term goals as well as important events, social activities or holidays when you won't be able to study. Don't feel that you have to get this exactly right now: you can always revise your goals in the light of events.

Six tips for successful planning

1. **Set yourself targets**. These give you something to aim at and allow you a regular sense of achievement when you reach them.
2. **Think about all your goals**. Make sure that your goals are sufficient: they must ensure that you achieve what you want to do.
3. **Be realistic**. If you set yourself targets that you are not capable of achieving, your motivation will be reduced rather than increased.
4. **Build flexibility into your schedule**. Don't expect that you will be able to keep to your timetable without a hitch. Something is likely to crop up to upset your planning, so make sure that you have scope to make some late adjustments.
5. **Don't overplan**. This can be an excuse for not starting important work. If your original targets turn out to be unrealistic, you can always revise your work schedule later.
6. **Monitor your progress**. Check whether you are keeping up with your work schedule and make any necessary adjustments if you fall behind.

From How to Succeed: Students' Guide

In pairs

Read the advice in the article 'Six tips for successful planning'. Now look at each other's monthly study planners and discuss whether you think the goals set down are sufficient, realistic and flexible. Can you suggest ways in which your partner's study plan could be improved?

Getting down to work

Do you find it difficult making the best use of your time when you get down to work? Nigel Roonie has some advice …

✦ **Choose study times that suit your learning style**. People work best at different times of day. If you work best in the morning, try to plan morning study sessions.

✦ **Use short periods of spare time**. As well as longer periods that you have set aside for studying, there will always be short periods of spare time – in the evening, say, or on the bus. All these periods add up, so use them constructively.

✦ **Get into a routine**. If you can, develop a routine, for example getting down to work at a particular time in the evening, or as soon as you get in from school. It is easier to start work if you are in the habit of studying at a particular time.

✦ **Identify priorities**. Think about which pieces of work need to be done first, and list them in order of priority. Then plan your time accordingly. Don't simply sit down to do 'two hours' work – you'll wonder where the time went.

✦ **Build variety into your work**. If you include a variety of activites – reading, writing, thinking and research – you'll find you can concentrate for longer periods and get more done.

✦ **Give yourself breaks**. Having regular short breaks actually increases your output of work because you return to work refreshed and with your concentration levels high. A break of 5 or 10 minutes every 45 minutes or so will help you work more effectively.

✦ **Break down your work into small manageable tasks**. Make a list of the tasks you need to do, and tick off each task as you complete it. This is good for planning and also for motivation, as you see that you are quickly reaching your goal.

✦ **Keep several tasks on the go at the same time**. If you find that you're making no progress with the work that you had planned, you can always return to it later. Choose something instead that you are more in the mood for.

✦ **Avoid distractions and interruptions**. Study in a place where there are no distractions, such as people talking or watching television. And don't allow anyone to interrupt you: if there's a phone call you can always explain that you are busy and that you will ring them back later.

✦ **Gather all the resources you need first**. Don't waste time by starting a piece of work only to find that you've left your notes behind, or that you haven't got a vital book, journal or piece of equipment.

✦ **Finally, MAKE A START**. We all find it difficult to get started, but try not to get distracted onto an unimportant task. Your work won't go away, and your stress and guilt will increase. If you get down to it you'll benefit from a great sense of achievement – and you'll get it done!

Get SMART

When you sit down to work you need to set precise goals that are SMART:

Specific
Measurable
Appropriate/adequate
Realistic
Time limited.

Specific: Work out precisely what you want to achieve in the time available, for example, 'Tonight I will plan my history assignment and identify my gaps in information ready for library time tomorrow.'

Measurable: It is useful to be able to check that you have done what you set out to do. 'Reading chapter 2 as part of my essay preparation' is specific, but it is only measurable if you make notes on the information relevant for your essay.

Appropriate/adequate: Make sure your goal is sufficient to cover what is required. If you need to hand in your essay tomorrow, the goal of today's work should be more than simply doing the reading for the essay!

Realistic: On the other hand, it is demoralising if you set yourself a goal that is impossible to achieve in the time that you have set aside. You should ask yourself what you can reasonably expect to achieve given the time and energy available.

Time limited: Every goal can usefully have a time limit attached to focus your energies and to allow you to review whether or not you have achieved it.

Adapted from *How to Succeed in Exams and Assessments*, by Penny Henderson

In groups

Read the articles 'Getting down to work' and 'Get SMART'. Discuss the advice given about making the best use of your time. Which do you think are the most helpful tips?

Role play

Role play a scene in which a young person complains to their parent that they just can't get down to work. They don't know where to start, they never seem to have the right materials at the right time, and they spend a lot of time worrying instead of studying.

Planning your revision

There are many different ways of approaching revision, but underlying all of them is careful planning and organisation. You will need to think about what to revise, when to revise it, and where and how to do it. This page looks at the 'what', 'when' and 'where' of revision; the material on page 17 is devoted to the 'how' – good methods of revision.

What to revise

First of all, you need to find out as much as you can about each examination that you are taking. This means looking at the syllabus and at past exam papers. The syllabus tells you the topics you must study, the form the exam will take and the marks that will be given for each part of the exam. Looking at past papers will give you a good idea of the kind of questions that are asked and which questions or topics come up regularly.

Use the syllabus and past papers to draw up a checklist of things that you need to be sure about before you plan your revision. Ask your teacher or course tutor if you are still unsure about the structure and requirements of any exam you are taking.

Finding out about the exam

You must be sure about the following things before you plan your revision:

✱ What is the time allowed for the exam?

✱ How many questions are you required to answer in that time?

✱ How much time are you recommended to spend on each question?

✱ What form do the questions take? (Essays, short answers, multiple choice …?)

✱ Do you have to answer the questions in a particular order?

✱ Can you take any aids such as a calculator, books, or a dictionary into the exam?

✱ Are there any compulsory questions?

✱ Are there any topics which you can safely leave out (for example, because you only have to do four out of eight questions)?

✱ Are the questions written in such a way that you need to know about more than one section of the course in order to answer them?

Adapted from *How to Succeed: Student's Guide*

On your own

Choose an exam that is coming up for you. Get hold of the syllabus and a recent exam paper and see if you can answer the questions in the panel above. If you can answer all of them you know exactly what the exam requires of you.

When to revise

Try to get into the habit of revising at regular times, and when you are at your most alert. Hopefully you will already have been used to planning your study sessions at times that suit your learning style (see page 15). The same applies when you revise.

As your exams approach you will need to draw up a revision calendar so that you can plan what work you are going to do, and when to do it. The article below explains how to do this.

Making a revision calendar

It's a good idea to draw up a revision calendar for the 10–12 weeks prior to the examinations. Follow these steps …

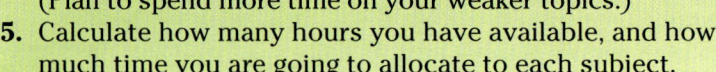

1. Pin a large calendar or year planner on the wall next to where you study.
2. Mark in the dates and times of your exams.
3. Mark in the dates and times of any other commitments, e.g. family outings and sports events.
4. Make a list of all the topics in each subject that you need to revise, and of how much time you think you need to spend on each topic. (Plan to spend more time on your weaker topics.)
5. Calculate how many hours you have available, and how much time you are going to allocate to each subject.
6. Decide on the order in which you are going to tackle your subjects and the topics within them.
7. Write on your calendar which subjects and topics you plan to revise each day. (Plan a variety of topics each day.)
8. Leave one or two revision slots blank in each week. You can use these for extra revision of a topic that you found difficult, or if you get behind schedule for any reason.
9. Make sure that your revision plan is geared to the structure and focus of the exams (see 'What to revise', left).
10. Make sure you leave yourself time for rest and leisure, particularly in the last few days before the exams.

Adapted from *Studywise 2*

In pairs

Following the steps outlined above, each draft a revision calendar. Discuss your calendars together and suggest any alterations that you think might improve them.

Have they left room for leisure activities?

In groups

Discuss what factors make an 'ideal' revision place. Does your revision place match this ideal? If not, what could you do to change it?

How to revise

You have probably already got a number of fat files of notes, handouts and marked assignments from various subjects, although some will be better organised than others. First of all you need to go through all this material and find out if there are any topics or areas of the course which you have covered in only a very sketchy way. If these are important topics, you need to find out more about them.

Whatever the present state of your notes, it is important that you make your own revision notes. Just *making* the notes is a form of revision, and you can use colours, symbols and abbreviations that are meaningful to you.

The article below suggests different ways in which you can make your revision notes.

From *How to Succeed in Exams and Assessments* by Penny Henderson

Extending and improving your notes

Good note-taking should reflect the purpose for which the notes will be used. Revision notes are an aid to memory, and a way of condensing a substantial amount of material into a form which you can readily recall in an exam.

Simply reading your notes over and over again will not help you to understand them, nor is it a helpful way to memorise the key points. Successful learning and memorising of material involves three stages: understanding, storing and recalling. You can:

- make summaries, condensing material from several sources;
- select and memorise key ideas and vivid examples;
- make lists of key words or definitions which will remind you of complex arguments;
- rewrite material in your own words, where you have not already done so;
- select and memorise quotable quotes.

You may find it helpful to use index cards as an aid to active revision. They can be a handy means of summarising notes, planning answers or noting down key themes and then practising your recall of them.

◑ In pairs

Work with someone who is doing the same course as you. Choose a topic and each study your notes on that topic and produce a set of revision cards. Use some of the suggestions in the article above, if they are appropriate. Then compare your revision cards. Have you found useful, effective ways of presenting the information? Finally, you can use the revision cards to test each other on the topic.

Active revision techniques

Apart from the basics of making notes and revision cards, here are some active revision techniques that you might try:

1. **Practising recall**. Try to learn information in a way which works well for you. If you have a strong visual memory, try to visualize the way that information appears on the pages of your notes. If you respond better to sounds than images, you could revise by making tapes of your refined revision notes and playing them over to yourself.

2. **Working with other students**. Students can benefit greatly from working together, testing each other, talking over what they believe to be the meaning of key terms, and so on. If you have a strong auditory memory this can be a particularly successful way of revising. It has the extra bonus of providing mutual encouragement and support.

3. **Putting yourself in the position of the examiner**. A key part of your revision strategy should be to review each section of your course from the standpoint of the examiner. Ask yourself what questions you would set if you wanted to test someone's understanding of this topic. If your teacher is setting the exam questions, think about which aspects of the course he or she has laid particular emphasis on.

4. **Practising exam questions**. When you feel that you have prepared sufficiently well, look at some sample questions and work out how you would tackle them in an exam. For most students, it is probably not a good use of revision time to write out full answers to individual questions, however, and then check back to see what else you might have included in your plan.

From *How to Succeed: Students' Guide*

Active revision in six simple steps

Step 1: Give your session a focus. Don't just sit down and wade through your notes again. Think about what specific question you want to be able to answer at the end of the revision session, and focus your revision on that.

Step 2: Read your notes carefully. Use a pencil or highlighter to underline or highlight important facts and key terms.

Step 3: Make revision cards. Using the underlined or highlighted passages, make revision cards. They can contain information, essential points, key ideas, definitions, examples and even diagrams.

Step 4: Study your revision cards and learn them. You can use any method that works for you, such as making audio tapes of you reading the cards, which you can listen to on your headset.

Step 5: Test yourself. Again, use any way that works, such as writing out the cards from memory, practising answering past papers in note form or in full, or getting a friend to test you.

Step 6: Check it. Look again at your revision cards to make sure that you got the facts right and didn't miss out anything important. Highlight these weaker areas on your revision cards, or rewrite the card to incorporate any new material.

⊕ In groups

Discuss the active revision techniques outlined in the two articles above. Which do you think are the most useful suggestions?

for your folder

Read Lisa's letter (below) and draft an answer.

Dear Mark, Exams are only six weeks off and I feel like giving up already. I spend hours reading my notes, but none of it is really going in. And I catch myself staring out of the window to escape from it all. What can I do?
Lisa

Coping with exams

Learning from the trial exams

Trial exams (or mocks) are useful ways of identifying your strengths and weaknesses. They tell you which subjects you are doing well in, and which subjects or topics you need to concentrate more on. A close review of your results in the trial exams will also highlight which techniques are letting you down.

Reviewing your results

Use this checklist of questions to help you to review your results and to identify the reasons why you didn't do as well as you had hoped in one of your subjects:

- Did you follow the instructions properly?
- Did you complete all the questions?
- Did you make the right choice of questions?
- Did you misunderstand some of the questions?
- Were some of your answers badly planned and illogical, because you rushed into writing them, instead of spending time thinking and planning?
- Did you answer some questions in too much detail and others in not enough detail?
- Did you miss out important points in some of your answers?
- Did you run out of time because you didn't plan carefully enough?
- Did you make careless mistakes because you didn't check your answers?
- Did your memory let you down because you hadn't done enough revision?
- Did you panic and start making silly mistakes?

From Studywise 2

On your own

Choose one of your subjects in which you felt you let yourself down, and go through the paper again, using the checklist (above) to help you analyse what you did wrong. Make a list of four things that you plan to do differently when you tackle the actual exam.

Coping with exam stress

It is quite normal to feel anxious and stressed before an examination. Indeed, a mild form of anxiety is actually good for us when we are under pressure, as it keeps us alert and makes us perform to the best of our ability. However, if someone is too anxious it can have the opposite effect – it stops them thinking straight (and even sleeping) and makes them panic and lose confidence.

Six ways of surviving exam pressure

1. **Learn to relax.** There are many relaxation techniques that may work for you, such as meditation and yoga. Your doctor may be able to suggest some, or you could get a book out of the library.

2. **Use visualisation.** Think of aspects of the exam that cause you to panic. Then relax and visualise (imagine) yourself overcoming the difficulties, one at a time, working up to the most fearful. End up with a picture of yourself doing the exam confidently.

3. **Remind yourself of past successes.** In whatever area you have been successful – exams in the same or other subjects, coursework, or any areas of school, sporting or home life – think of your successes. This will remind you that you are competent and can succeed.

4. **Share your worries.** Talking to friends and family, or even your teacher, can be a great benefit. They can be a source of support and advice, and make you realise that you're not alone in your anxiety. Friends who generally do well in exams can also give you practical advice.

5. **Prepare early for the exam.** Leaving your revision to the last minute is bound to make you worried that you won't be properly prepared for the exam.

6. **Take some exercise.** Can you spend the afternoon before the exam playing tennis or swimming or taking some other form of exercise? Rather than being a waste of studying time, it will relax you and help you sleep well. It's a far better use of time than last-minute cramming.

In groups

1. How do you feel as you approach an exam? Discuss your fears and worries with other members of the group.

2. Discuss the article 'Six ways of surviving exam pressure'. Which are the most useful pieces of advice? Do you use any other stress-busting methods that you can share with the group?

Before the exam

So you've done as much preparation as you can, you've worked on your anxiety, and your exam is tomorrow. Here is a checklist of the final, practical steps that you can take to prepare for the exam.

- ✔ Check the correct date and time of the exam.
- ✔ Ensure that you know where the exam is being held.
- ✔ Check what equipment you need, and whether you have to provide it yourself:
  a) pens – including cartridges or a refill
  b) pencils
  c) rubber
  d) watch
  e) calculator – plus spare battery
  f) any other equipment.

Try to get a good night's sleep, and on the day of the exam allow yourself plenty of time to get to school. Don't arrive too early, however, as all the waiting around and conversations about revision will make you more nervous.

for your folder

Draw up a list of 'Dos and Don'ts Before an Exam'. Swap your list with a partner's, and improve yours if you can. Then copy it into your folder.

Taking examinations

What should I do when I get into the exam?

▲ When you get to your desk, check that you have all the equipment you need. If anything is missing, ask the invigilator for it before the exam begins.

▲ Listen carefully to any instructions given by the invigilator. Do not turn over the exam paper until you are told to.

▲ Fill in the necessary personal details on the answer booklet.

▲ Read the instructions on the exam paper carefully, and scan all the questions.

▲ Decide which questions you are going to answer. Make sure that these include all the compulsory questions, and that you are doing the appropriate number of questions in each section.

▲ Decide the order in which you are going to answer the questions. Start with your 'best' question, as that will give you confidence to tackle the others.

▲ Work out a time plan such as the one below, by dividing your time carefully between the questions. During the exam, check occasionally that you are sticking to your time plan.

Reading time	9.30–9.45
Q.1	9.45–10.15
Q.4	10.15–10.45
Q.7	10.45–11.15
Final check	11.15–11.30

Adapted from How to Succeed: Students' Guide

Presentation and layout

Lay out your work as simply as possible. Imagine a tired examiner reading the fiftieth answer to the same question. They need help to see easily what you mean. You can provide this by using:

● short sentences
● separate paragraphs for each new point
● clear diagrams.

Focus your attention on quality of response more than on quantity. Provided that you say all that is necessary in order to fully answer the question, you are unlikely to gain additional marks for length.

It can be useful to leave a gap of several lines between paragraphs of an essay, or at the end, so that when you come back to read it through you can insert any points which have occurred to you later, or, even more important, add in a sentence to make clear the relevance of the material in the paragraph.

From How to Succeed in Exams and Assessments by Penny Henderson

If things start to go wrong...

Running out of time

If you begin to run out of time, stop and re-plan the rest of the exam. Ask yourself:

❂ Could I manage to do a basic answer for all questions?
❂ Can I quickly finish the question I am currently working on?
❂ Could I be more concise?
❂ Could I finish in note form, or show the relevant steps in a calculation, even if I do not have time to carry them out?

Bear in mind that you must always answer the number of questions asked for. It will always be easier to gain a few quick marks for a new answer, even if it is very short or in note form, than to squeeze a few additional marks out of an answer which is already of a reasonable standard.

Panicking

If you can't get started, or lose your nerve in the middle, try one or more of the following:

❂ Shut your eyes and take some deep breaths, sigh, allow yourself to picture someone who thinks you are OK; imagine their voice saying something encouraging.
❂ If you panic because you are stuck with a question, leave it and work on your plan for the next one.
❂ Go to the loo. You can feel much more relaxed just by getting out of the exam room for a few minutes.
❂ Take a complete rest for three minutes, daydream, relax. Then sit up very straight so there is room to breathe deep into your lungs, and begin work again.

From How to Succeed in Exams and Assessments by Penny Henderson

Planning your answers

When you are tackling questions that require longer answers, such as essays, it is essential to spend a few minutes planning your answer so it will be coherent and logical.

A step-by-step approach:

1. Look again at the questions, focusing on the key words, in order that you understand the type of answer that is required. For example, does it require an analytical or factual answer? Does the question provide a structure for your answer?

2. Take a piece of spare paper and do a brainstorm, noting the points you are going to make in your answer in any order, as they come into your mind.

3. Look through your list of key points and decide on the best order in which to put them. Don't write the list out again, simply write numbers beside each point to indicate in which paragraph or section of the answer you should put it. Make sure that the point that you put last is an appropriate conclusion to the answer.

4. Think of a suitable introductory sentence or paragraph and start writing.

Planning your answer will keep you focused on answering the question, help you to think clearly and make you feel more confident and calm.

From Studywise 2

In groups

Read and discuss the advice that is given on this page about how to tackle your exams. Which are the most helpful pieces of advice?

4 Managing Your Money

Handling your money

Money. Love it or hate it, we all need it – and most of us probably wish we had more of it. The most important thing is to work out how to control your money so that it doesn't end up controlling you.

Attitudes to money

How well you control your money will depend on your attitude towards it.

In pairs

Consider the points of view expressed by the six people (right). Which view (or views) do you think is the most sensible and why?

Planning a budget

You never know when you're going to want that extra book, CD or a night out. So draw up a budget plan. This is how you do it:

1 Break down your incoming money, allowance or wages for part-time work for each week or month so that you know in advance what your income is going to be.

2 List those things which you need to pay for on a regular basis. For example, clothes, stationery or travelling costs.

3 Subtract the costs (2) from your income (1). This is the spare cash that you have left for entertainment, or possibly even for saving.

Planning your budget in this way will ensure that you run your money, rather than the other way round. You'll know how much extra you've got to spend on yourself, and you won't feel guilty about having a good time.

'I know exactly how much I spend each month – and what I spend it on. I make a list so that I can keep an eye on my spending.'
Jamill

'I don't know where my money goes – it just seems to vanish.'
Tyrone

'I never seem to have any money. I get an allowance but when I've paid for going out and new clothes, I never have anything left for extra things.'
Sam

'I love clothes and can't wait to get the latest outfit. I don't save but my parents always help me out.'
Louise

'I'm a good swimmer and I have to spend money on training and kit. I don't have much spare cash – but I manage to pay for important things first.'
Tom

'I spend too much on clothes, really. I hang around with a group who wear designer clothes all the time. I feel I have to keep up.'
Charlotte

In pairs

Discuss what you have learnt from writing your money diary about your spending habits. Were you surprised by your spending in any particular area? Do you feel worried about the amounts you spend on particular things?

What to do with your spare cash

So you've got some spare cash. What's the best thing to do with it? There are lots of options. You can spend it and treat yourself to something that you've always wanted. You can get someone to buy you some lottery tickets and hope that you'll win a fortune. Or you can save it.

If you decide to save it, you can put it into a bank account or a building society account, where it will earn you interest. You can buy premium bonds or national savings certificates. Or you can buy items such as stamps or coins which might increase in value.

For research

Find out all you can about different ways of saving and investing money. Then, imagine that you have £1000 to save or to invest. Decide what you would do with the money and explain your decision to the rest of the class in a class discussion.

for your folder

Write a money diary for a week, taking note of how much you spend and on what. Present your figures in columns headed according to the area of spending.

On-line credit for teenagers

Is on-line credit a new way of helping teenagers learn how to handle their money, or a new way of getting teenagers to part with their money? Four people give their views on the introduction of an internet credit card for young people, designed to make it easier for them to spend their money on the web.

The Question: A new internet credit card for kids will make it easier for children to spend their pocket money on the web. Is this a good idea?

Brian Beausoleil
Managing Director Splash Plastic

We developed the card to overcome the risks of shopping on line and have focussed on safety, security and privacy. The card can only be used at selected websites that sell appropriate products for the teenage market such as CDs, games, research material and fashion. There are also no risks of over spending or getting into debt. Children are already using pre-paid cards for mobile phones and are learning how to get most value out of them through text-messaging. Children can be independent from their parents because there are no risks involved.

Verdict: **Yes**

Gill Hind
Education department, Financial Services Authority

Shopping on the net is seductive, easy and instant and parents may not feel comfortable letting their children buy things they haven't even seen. Shopping this way allows children to indulge in buying on a whim and with children not even seeing the money, they may not learn its value. On the plus side, this card won't encourage living off credit because it only allows children to spend what they've got. Used sensibly, it's good practice at using debit and credit cards for spending, which is mainly what they'll continue doing as adults.

Verdict: **Maybe**

Tom Hadfield
Student and net user, 17

The Internet will make it easier for young people to spend money, and it will seem a much more usual place to buy things to my generation than it was to my parents'. Of course there are dangers in that, and some parents won't like the idea of a credit card for kids, or that their children can buy things on the net that they can't at the shops. But I'd say this is an opportunity – the answer isn't to restrict them, it's to teach them about responsible spending. In any case, these cards aren't strictly credit cards at all. Every teenager will want one, and I want one too.

Verdict: **Yes**

Wendy Elms
Mother of four children aged 9, 12, 14 and 16

Children today are lazy enough already, and this will be another reason for them not to get up off their chairs and get a bit of exercise. Shopping on the net draws them in and can easily become an obsession, so I'd be very wary of anything that encourages it. Although I take the point about the credit on the card, there's still the risk they will just blow all the money at once – and because it's just a card it won't help them learn the value of real cash. It's just another pressure on parents, isn't it? Mine already go on about needing their mobile phone credits topped up.

Verdict: **No**

In pairs

1. Discuss the views expressed above. Do you agree with the points made by the people questioned? Give your reasons.
2. Make a list of the advantages and disadvantages of internet credit cards for children. Try to agree on three key points for and against.

Feedback

Present your views on the internet credit card to the class.

Money matters

What happens when you lend money to your friends and they won't give it back?

'She owes me money'

About a year ago my 'best' friend was going out with a lad from school. She wanted to buy him a chain, and borrowed the money for it from me. The trouble is, I need the money back, but every time I mention it she always says, 'I know, you'll get it back.'

When she asked me to lend her it she told me she had a job and could pay me back a bit each week, but I haven't seen a single penny. I know she can afford to give me the money as her family is fairly well off, especially compared to mine. She even had the cheek to come down and boast about a top she'd bought for £25 that she didn't even need. Why couldn't she have given that money to me? I just don't know what to do.

Tricia Kreitman replies:

Lending or borrowing money is always a dodgy business. It causes ill-feeling and resentment and breaks up many friendships and even families. It's no good being wiser after the event, but I can't promise there's anything you can do now to get the money back.

Different people have very different attitudes to money.

When you're hard up, every penny counts and you tend to be more responsible about how you spend what you have. Sadly, if you've never had to budget and your parents have bailed you out of anything remotely resembling a financial crisis, it's easy to develop a somewhat casual attitude towards the stuff.

Your only chance of getting the money back is to sit her down and tell her exactly how upset you are about this and how important that money is to you. She may cough up immediately, or she may keep putting it off. In that case, Plan B in my book would be to embarrass her in front of her family and friends by pointing out her bad debts. No, you are unlikely to remain friends after this, but you're not exactly matey at the moment, are you?

Having said all this, you may not get the money back. You can't force somebody to settle a private debt, but you can make it quite clear just how disgusted you are with their behaviour.

 **In groups**

1. Discuss Tricia Kreitman's advice on how to deal with a situation in which you have lent someone some money and they haven't paid it back. Say why you agree or disagree with her advice.

2. Study the letters (below) from other people about money matters and discuss how you would reply to them. Then share your suggestions in a class discussion.

'If I want things, I have to earn money to pay for them'

My mum always used to give me pocket money regularly, but I never had enough for all the things I wanted. So I went and got myself a part-time job.

Now that I'm earning, she's stopped giving me any money. She says if I want things it's up to me to earn enough to pay for them. I'm no better off now than I was when I wasn't working.

What really gets me is that she still gives my younger sister money. What do you think I should do? I feel like packing in my job.

— Sam, 15

'My sister's run up this huge debt'

When she was 18, the bank gave my sister a credit card. She thought it was great and went on a spending spree, buying herself all sorts of new things. The trouble is she's run up this huge bill. She says she's having to pay back so much in interest every month that the bill never gets any smaller.

She used to be so happy-go-lucky and was going out all the time. Now she's moody and depressed. I'm worried that she'll go and do something stupid in order to get the money. She's frightened to tell our mum about it, because our parents have always said that once we get to 18 it's up to us to look after ourselves. Is there anything I can do to help her?

— Amelia, 16

'Everything's so expensive'

My parents give me an allowance and expect me to pay for everything – my clothes, my toiletries, my stationery, even for repairs to my bike. My problem is that I never have enough, because everything's so expensive.

I have to keep a record of my phone calls and pay for them. I never go out because I can't afford to. So I spend a lot of time on my computer, but now they say I'm using it so much that I must pay for the cost of using it.

They say that they are teaching me the value of money and how to handle it. But I'm getting to the end of my tether. Are they being fair? Please help me.

— Jackie, 15

From *Mizz* magazine

A place of your own

Many teenagers dream of leaving home as soon as they are 16 and finding a place of their own. But, **says Erica Stewart**, you need to think carefully before trying to go it alone.

Wouldn't it be nice to have a place of your own, where you and some of your friends could live and do as you liked without having your parents on your back all the time? Sounds great, doesn't it? But before you go rushing out of the door, you need to stop and think about how much it's all going to cost.

There's the rent for a start. Rooms don't come cheap and, even if there are several of you sharing a flat, you can find the rent takes a hefty chunk out of your income. Then there's the household bills that you'll have to pay for all the water, electricity and gas that you use.

Next, there are all the essentials – your food and the toiletries you use. And, of course, other basic things that you may have taken for granted when living at home, such as washing-up liquid, shoe polish and toilet paper. It all adds up.

And what about transport? You may be able to walk or cycle to work or college. But it's often hard to find a place close to where you're working or studying, so there are usually fares to be budgeted for.

By the time you've paid for all these things, there may be little or nothing left to spend on your leisure – on things like going to a club or to see the latest film. What seemed like a good idea at first may not seem so appealing when you've stopped to count the cost.

Paula's problem

Paula left home ten weeks ago and went to live with three of her friends. They are sharing a flat together. Paula's problem is that she doesn't seem to be able to make ends meet.

When she was living at home, Paula never had any money left by the end of the week. She was always having to borrow money from her mum.

Now that she's away from home the situation is worse. Money just seems to slip through her fingers.

At home her parents used to let her live rent free, but she gave her mum £15 a week towards her food. Then she'd spend the rest of her money on clothes and make-up and going out. If she saw a CD she wanted she was always able to get it. If she couldn't afford it, there was always Mum – or even Dad!

Things are different now. Besides the rent to pay, she has to pay for all her own food and £15 doesn't go very far. Then, of course, there is her share of the gas and electricity bills. There's no phone in the flat, so she has to rely on her mobile. But it's so expensive. At home, there was a phone which she could use as much as she liked, and Dad paid the bill.

'I didn't realise that it would cost so much,' she says. 'I've never got any money. My friends seem to manage better than I do. But they won't ever lend me any. They say I ought to be more careful and that I shouldn't buy so many clothes or use my mobile so much.

'I'm getting fed up. I'm thinking of going back home. I don't want to have to do that now that I'm old enough to live on my own. But I don't seem to have any choice.'

⊕ **In groups**

1. Discuss what you learn from the article by Erica Stewart about all the costs you have to budget for when you have a place of your own.

2. Talk about Paula's problem. Has she got a choice? What advice would you give her?

◖ **In pairs**

Role play a scene in which a teenager tries to persuade a 16-year-old friend, who is determined to leave home and find a place of their own, that they need to think through what they are doing, because they might find it impossible to find a place they can afford.

"Young people don't know when they are well off. If they've got a roof over their heads and their parents are paying for their keep, it's far better for them to stick it out rather than to try to go it alone. I should know. I left home when I was sixteen and I haven't had a proper home since.

Danny, 26, who is homeless and living on the street

for your folder Imagine that Paula has written to ask your advice on how to plan a budget. Write your reply to her.

5

Thinking About Careers

Assessing your personal qualities

When you are considering what career you might follow, it's important not to rush your decision. It's also important to think about what sort of person you are and what skills and talents you have.

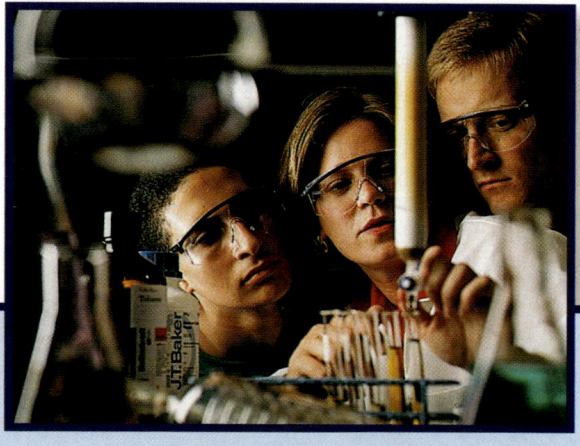

Starting to think about a career

A few people make up their minds about their careers very early on in their lives. They may be influenced by their parents' careers or by another adult whose job sounds interesting. They may be impressed by something they have read or seen – in books, films or advertising, all of which create job images. It is a good idea to talk to adults who are actually doing the type of jobs you are interested in. They may give you a very different picture from the one you get from the media.

It can be hard to imagine yourself in the world of work. When you leave school you really become part of the adult world and people expect to be able to trust and rely on you. How can you make a career decision when your only experience has been school life? Which is why it's a good idea to take the opportunity to see what the world of work is like by getting a part-time job or doing some work experience.

If you feel uncertain about your skills and talents, take time to decide what is best for you. Don't be pushed into something that you don't want to do, just because somebody else suggests that it would be a good idea for you to do it.

People's interests change, especially when you're young. So it's sensible to keep an open mind for as long as you can. You never know how your views might change. And the job you're thinking of doing now might change in the future too. Be aware that you may need to adapt and retrain for new technologies as they come along.

Some people are lucky enough to have a burning ambition that carries them through until they achieve a goal. Don't worry if this isn't you. Lots of people fall into their chosen career by accident or decide very late on. However, it does help to have some idea about what you think might suit you.

To begin with, it's a good idea to assess yourself. Find out what you think you're good at and what you're not so hot on. Everyone has weaknesses, the clever part is choosing a career where they won't matter.

Your personal qualities

Knowing what your personal qualities are will help you to choose a career that suits you.

adventurous   aggressive   assertive   calm   caring
conscientious   courageous   dependable   determined
disorganised   easy-going   enthusiastic   fair
flexible   forgetful   generous   hard-working
honest   humorous   imaginative   level-headed
loyal   optimistic   outgoing   passive   patient
persevering   polite   self-confident   shy   sincere
stubborn   sympathetic   tactful   tolerant

for your folder

On your own study the list of words above and decide which of these qualities – or their opposites – belong to you. Be honest and self-critical. Most people have a mixture of strengths and weaknesses. The more you recognise your own strengths and weaknesses, the more it will help you to choose a career that is suitable for you.

When you have made a list of your qualities, write a statement about yourself similar to the statements that Morris and Serena wrote about themselves (right).

I'm outgoing. I get on well with people of all ages and I've really enjoyed my part-time job working in our local supermarket. I'm fairly well-organised and I'm co-operative – I don't mind people telling me what to do. I think I'd fit well into a shop or an office, so I'm considering either staying on and doing a course that will develop my business skills or finding a job that will give me some training. Morris

People tell me I've got a strong personality, because I always say what I think and stick up for my beliefs; because I've got a stubborn streak. I'm very determined and I want to do something that will make a contribution to society. I think I could cope with the kinds of situations you'd have to face if you were a fire officer or a police officer, so that's what I'm thinking of doing at present. But I plan to stay on and get some academic qualifications first and then see if I still feel the same in two years' time. Serena

In pairs

Show your written statement to a partner and discuss together **a)** what you have learned about your personal qualities, and **b)** what sorts of career might be suitable for someone with your qualities.

Identifying your skills

Thinking about what you're good at and why will also help you when trying to decide on a career that will suit you.

Everyone has skills. Being skilled doesn't just mean things like being able to read and write and pass exams. There are thousands of different skills in life – from being able to find your way round the internet to knowing how to bait a fishing-line. The activities on this page are designed to help you to identify different skills and to think about which careers require these kind of skills.

Adapted from *Keep Your Options Open* by Vivienne Neale

Types of skills

Skills can be divided into five main areas:

1 People skills
   * communication
   * inspiration
   * negotiation
   * appreciation
   * delegation
   * determination
   * advising

2 Thinking skills
   * evaluating
   * problem solving
   * prioritising
   * weighing up evidence and alternatives

3 Using information
   * memorising
   * researching
   * record keeping
   * calculating
   * classifying/organising information
   * observing

4 Helping people get things done
   * coordinating and liaising
   * overseeing
   * planning
   * recognising other people's talents/skills

5 Seeing things from a different angle
   * finding alternatives
   * thinking laterally
   * flair and imagination
   * seeing potential
   * finding links
   * seeing relationships/connections

In pairs

Think about these broad skill areas. Discuss the kinds of employment that would make best use of the skills in each area. (Think in general terms for this activity, not of your own skills.)

for your folder

Think of a situation where you have used and developed skills in any of the areas listed above. Then write a statement about the skills you have and how you might use them in a career, similar to the statements that Joe, Teresa and Sasha wrote (below).

I'm a very practical person. I'm good at looking at diagrams and understanding how things work. I've also got a lot of patience. You have to have with a hobby like mine. My grandfather was a watchmaker and he's taught me how to take apart and assemble old watches. It's fascinating – like doing a complicated puzzle. I'm hoping to find a career that will enable me to use these skills. Joe

I've got a good memory and my science teacher says I've got good research skills. I'm good at making observations and classifying and organising information. I think I'd like to do laboratory work of some kind. Teresa

I'm not very academic, but I think I'm good with people. I got on very well with my Nan (my great-grandmother) and I used to help Mum to care for her when she was ill. I think I'd be quite good at the practical side of care work, so long as I didn't have to do anything too technical. Sasha

For research

1. Matching the skills you need in order to do different jobs will help to tell you about future career choices. Use the careers library to find out what skills are needed for different jobs. As well as looking in books and leaflets, use CDs, videos and the internet to find out what skills particular jobs require.

2. Choose three different jobs and list the skills that are considered necessary for them. Do you think you have the right skills or the potential to develop the skills needed for these jobs?

Feedback

Report your findings from your research in a class discussion about the skills you need to develop for particular careers.

Investigating Careers

Before you choose a particular career, you need to find out all you can about what the job involves.
The more information you have about a job, the clearer it will become whether or not it's a job to suit you.
So what's the key information you need to find out? **Erica Stewart** *explains what you need to know.*

First and foremost, you need to establish exactly what activities you'd be doing in a particular job. Many people have a general idea of what certain jobs entail. For example, a surveyor examines buildings to determine their condition and value, but what exactly do they do in a normal day at work? You probably know that an optician deals with people's eyesight, supplying them with glasses and contact lenses. But did you know that there are actually two types of opticians, each doing different jobs? Ophthalmic opticians are people who are qualified to examine the eyes and to prescribe and supply spectacles and contact lenses, whereas dispensing opticians can supply and fit spectacle frames and lenses but are not qualified to examine eyes. If you're interested in being an optician, you need to find out exactly what each type of optician does.

Visit the workplace

The best way to find out what someone actually does is to talk to a person who is doing that job. You may even be able to visit them at work. If you do, take a close look at the workplace. Whatever job you're interested in, you need to know where you'll be working. You need to ask yourself: Is it the sort of environment I'd be happy to spend eight hours a day in? Will I be working on my own or with other people? Will I have to motivate myself or will there be a supervisor or manager near by who will be keeping a close eye on me all the time?

Qualifications

Nowadays, most careers require you to have qualifications. So find out what basic qualifications you need to start the job and where you can get the necessary training, education or experience for that type of work. Ask what the career structure is. Can you start at the bottom and work your way up, getting the necessary training as you do so? Or do most people who choose such a career go to college first, get their qualifications and then start work? If that's the case, there may be certain subjects that you need to go on studying or a particular course that you need to apply for.

Restrictions

It's important, too, before you get too interested in a career, to discover whether there are any particular restrictions about that career. For example, do you have to be over a certain age, or are there any medical restrictions, such as not being colour blind?

There may also be restricted opportunities. There may be no openings in that particular career in the area where you and your parents live. For example, some jobs are only found in large cities. Others are only available in certain parts of the country where particular companies are located. There may also be a lot of competition for that type of job. Certain careers are highly competitive, with a few qualified people competing for only a few jobs.

Rewards

You need to know what the rewards are for the career you are considering. Some careers offer high financial rewards. In others, the rewards may be in terms of personal fulfilment and job satisfaction rather than in a high salary.

Finally, once you have collected all the necessary information, think about the skills and abilities you need for that type of work and whether you would find the work satisfying. Researching a career thoroughly before you decide to take it up can help you to avoid starting something and then giving it up because you find out that it's not the job you thought it was going to be.

In pairs

Discuss what you learn from Erica Stewart's article and make a list of all the information you need to find out about a career which you are interested in. Each choose a career which currently interests you. Then work together to compile a job factsheet for the two jobs, consisting of all the information you can discover about that particular job.

In groups

Discuss what Kerry's job involves (right) and why she likes it, and say what you would like and dislike about her job. Say why you think such a job would or would not suit you.

for your folder Interview someone aged between 16 and 24 about their job. Write a short statement about what it involves and why they chose it and say why you think a similar job would or would not suit you.

What My Job Is Like

Kerry Astley is 19. She works as a receptionist/administrator's clerk at the Saltash Health Centre in Cornwall and has passed NVQ Level 3 in business administration.

There's a rota system here so I do a lot of different jobs – dealing with telephone enquiries, in-coming and out-going mail, printing out prescriptions and getting them signed by a doctor as well as lots of filing duties and attending to requests from the doctors. I also register new patients, call them in for a new patient check and process the subsequent claims. There is always a lot to take in, a lot to learn.

Patients can sometimes be extremely vague and I have to refer quickly to their notes while I'm on the phone. It's a lot to juggle but everything has to be totally accurate because we are dealing with people's health.

What I like about my job is that every day is different and there is always plenty to do. I enjoy the combination of office work and helping people in a medical situation. Eventually I want to be a practice manager.

Applying for a Job

Once you have decided to apply for a job, your first task is usually to persuade the employer to interview you. Here is some advice and information about how to do so.

The first stage
To see whether it is worth calling you for interview, an employer may ask you to fill in an application form, send a CV or simply phone for more information.

Application forms
Many employers use application forms as the first stage, sometimes asking questions that require mini-essays in reply, such as:
- Give details of your main extracurricular interests. What have you contributed and what have you got out of them?
- Have you ever been in a situation where you have had to motivate people?

These questions may look difficult, but recruiters are not expecting the earth. This is your first job, after all. Use the personal statement section of your NRA to look for clues to help you answer them.
- Have you had a part-time job? Did you have responsibility for cash, or deal with difficult customers? (Demonstrating responsibility and customer care.)
- Are you in any sports teams? (Showing teamwork and/or leadership.)

There are lots of other examples you could give.

Tips
- Do read all the instructions first.
- Do make a copy of the form and use that to practise on in your best handwriting.
- Do check your spelling.
- Do photocopy the completed form – it will help you to remember what you wrote if you are called for interview.
- Don't make alterations and crossings-out.
- Don't give false information.
- Don't run out of space (a good reason for practising on an exact copy first).
- Don't use ink that isn't blue or black.
- Don't include relatives as references.

Letters of application
If you are not asked to complete an application form, you may have to put all the relevant information in a letter.
- Make sure you clearly state the title of the job for which you are applying and where you first read or heard about it.
- Be neat, accurate and honest. Use unlined paper (if writing by hand you can use a guide underneath.) It is OK to type – unless an advertisement clearly states, 'Apply in own handwriting.'
- Make sure that you start with your address, phone number and the date.
- End with 'Yours sincerely' if you are writing to a named person, and 'Yours faithfully' if you began 'Dear Madam' or 'Dear Sir'.
- Remember to sign your letter and print your name underneath.

Speculative letters
If you have a particular employer in mind, it can be worth writing on the off-chance that there might be a vacancy coming up. Your letter should be a concise combination of an application form and a CV and should:
- include your reasons for wanting the job
- demonstrate your enthusiasm
- show what steps you have taken to find out about the work.

Telephone applications
A job advertisement may ask you to phone the employer. This could be to request an application form, or the phone call may turn into a mini-interview. Remember:
- try to phone from somewhere private
- have a list of your qualifications to hand
- keep a pen and pencil ready in case you have to write anything or take notes
- be prepared – some people have been asked 'interview' questions at this point.

Curriculum Vitae (CV)
If you are making a number of applications for jobs, it is worth preparing a CV. This is a summary of information about yourself and it is something that you can use repeatedly – so it is worth making several copies. (For advice on how to prepare a CV, see page 28.)

Adapted from Job Book 2001

In pairs
Each draft the mini-essays you would write if asked to give details of your extracurricular activities, saying what you have contributed and what you have got out of them. Then read what your partner has written and comment on it, and if appropriate suggest ways in which they could improve it. Then repeat the exercise, this time writing about any situations in which you have had to show initiative and responsibility.

for your folder Study the advert (right), which appeared in the *Newtown Gazette* on 3 September 2001. Write a letter of application for the post.

Presenting your best side

Serena Pym offers advice on how to prepare your curriculum vitae.

Having a CV is a prerequisite for getting any job. But that doesn't mean you should treat it with indifference or as a necessary evil. Your CV is your first opportunity to make the right impression on a potential employer and as such, it is wise to make sure you get it right.

Presentation

Your CV needs to be clear and easy to read. It is a business document so it should look professional, although it is not necessary to spend hundreds of pounds getting it produced. Correctly typed or word processed but well laid out is fine. And do make sure you get someone to check it for spelling errors.

The length of the document is important. You don't want to bore your reader. It is important to bear in mind that he or she may have to read hundreds of CVs in response to a job ad, so make sure that yours is always kept to two pages maximum.

Purpose

The purpose of a CV is to give a brief, accurate description of who you are. It is an introduction to you, what you have done and where your interests lie. Whoever is reading it should be able to build up a picture of you, but will then need to interview you to simply confirm, or perhaps alter, their view. Remember that the person receiving your CV will never have met you, so it needs to convey your capabilities, experience and background.

By the time the recipient has finished reading the document, they should have a pretty good overview of your personal background, education and qualifications, work experience and any other relevant interests which add a dimension to your personality or which enhance your skills. To ensure that your CV is easy to read try to keep each of these sections separate on the page.

What the CV should cover

Personal background. The first page should start with your personal details: name, address, date of birth and a telephone number where you can be contacted.

Education and qualifications. Next give details of your education, including where you have studied, and any qualifications you have gained, or courses you have completed and exam results which you are waiting for.

Work experience. The next section should give details of any work experience. Be concise but give details of exactly what position you had and what the job involved.

Personal interests. Finally, include sections giving details of your extracurricular activities, any other key skills you have and your leisure activities. It can sometimes be difficult to see the relevance of including these 'personal interests' sections. But they have their purpose. The interests you follow give an indication of your personality and possibly highlight personal qualities which you may not have demonstrated elsewhere. They can also spark interest with an interviewer who may share your interest in a particular activity. You may have achieved recognition in your personal life – perhaps as a Duke of Edinburgh Award winner, or by representing your school, college or county at sport. Perhaps you do voluntary work, sing regularly in a choir or are a scout or guide. Details of this nature should all be included.

The translation of Curriculum Vitae from Latin means 'the course of one's life'. Your CV needs to take its reader through the course of your life, signposting the skills and experience gained along the way.

Adapted from an article by Serena Pym in Streetwyse

Tania Jones

Personal Information

Date of birth: 14/06/86
Address: 69 Tree Avenue, Greenborough, Oldtown XZ1 1JK
Tel: 00678 101202

Education and qualifications

Greenborough Comprehensive School, 1997–2002

GCSEs: English Language, Maths, Double Science, French, History, Art, Technology (awaiting results)

Employment experience

June 2001: Work experience, organised by school, in sales and marketing department of Bradley Technoparts, gaining experience of data entry

2001–present: Part-time sales assistant at Harrison's Bakery where I am responsible for serving customers and operating the till

Extracurricular activities

August 2000–August 2001 Member of Greenborough Young Environmentalist group, involved in converting a derelict site into a children's play area

2001–2002 Year 11 School Council representative

Leisure interests

I enjoy a range of sports and have represented the school at netball, athletics and tennis. In January 2002 I came 3rd in the County Under16 Cross-Country.

I play the trumpet in the school orchestra and I am a member of the Greenborough Community Brass Band, which was featured in the TV programme 'Brass Bands of Britain'.

Referees

Ms K. Cross, headteacher, Greenborough Comprehensive School, Middle Lane, Oldtown XZ3 4ER

Mr L. Harrison, manager, Harrison's Bakery, 10 Main Street, Oldtown XZ5 7TY

---

for your folder Use a word processor to draft your CV. Show it to a friend. Discuss whether you have left out anything important and ask them if they can think of any ways of improving the layout.

How to do well at interviews

Job interviews needn't be the daunting experience they're supposed to be. If you go in well prepared and feeling positive, they can be a chance to show the employer they've just met the right person for the job.

A good way of approaching an interview is to imagine the employer actually wants to give you the job – otherwise they wouldn't have invited you in the first place. While the employer is trying to find out about you, this is your chance to find out about the company and the job or training on offer.

Before the interview

✔ Look at any booklets, recruitment literature or websites produced by the company itself.
✔ Talk to people who work there.
✔ Read what you wrote in your application.
✔ Think of some questions you might be asked – not just easy ones – and try to work out some answers.
✔ Write down a list of questions you would like to ask – and take it with you.
✔ Do a mock interview at home or at school.

On the day of your interview

✔ Get there in plenty of time.
✔ Take trouble with your appearance. Wear something smart – blouse and skirt, jacket and tie.
✔ When you are called into the interview room, smile and wait to be seated.

What sort of questions to expect

✔ An experienced interviewer will try to put you at ease by asking the easy questions first, possibly enquiring about your coursework or your interests.
✔ Think before you speak, and answer clearly, fully and honestly. Don't be afraid to say if you don't understand a question.
✔ Try not to fidget, and do make an effort to look the interviewer in the eye. If the interview is conducted by a panel, talk to the questioner, but look at the others from time to time as you are answering.

Questions you may be asked

✔ Why did you apply for this position?
✔ What do you consider are your strengths/weaknesses?
✔ Why should we hire you in particular?
✔ Where do you see yourself in five years' time?
✔ Have you any questions? (Have some ready. This makes you look interested. But if they've all been answered – say so, 'I was going to ask about x and y but you have already covered that, thank you,' sounds much better than a simple 'no'.)

From Job Book 2001

Communicating Well

Speaking

The only way to discover how you come across when you're answering questions in an interview is to listen to yourself. Once the initial shock of the unrecognisable sound has passed, analyse precisely how you come across:

✧ Do you speak too loudly or in an inaudible mousy squeak?
✧ Do you tend to over-talk, gabbling on when a single sentence would suffice?
✧ Is the pitch of your voice varied enough to make what you have to say sound interesting?
✧ Do you speak clearly? Is it easy to make out what you say?
✧ Is your talk overloaded with ums and ahs?
✧ Do all your answers begin in the same way, with the same word, 'Well, …?

Listen to recordings objectively and practise improving the way you convey information to listeners.

Body Language

Pre-interview nervousness is to be expected – it may be distinctly useful, adding an edge of excitement that will invigorate the interview. It is not helpful if it leaves the interviewee looking cowed and terror-stricken. Craven posture is not going to inspire confidence.

A few simple pointers:

✧ Keep your arms unfolded; folding them across your chest is an unwelcoming, defensive gesture.
✧ Practise sitting so that you look neither too stiff nor so relaxed that you seem unconcerned or uninterested.
✧ Smile when you greet your interviewer, but a continuous, unwavering Cheshire Cat grin is disconcerting and unnatural.
✧ Don't hurry. Take your time to settle yourself so that once the interview begins you are quite unselfconscious about posture. This way the interviewer will not be distracted and both interviewer and interviewee can concentrate on what needs to be said.

From Jobfinder by Christine Ingham

In pairs

Study the articles on this page. Discuss what you have learned from them about how to prepare for interviews and how to create a good impression in an interview. Draw up a list of 'Ten top tips for interviewees'.

Role play

Each choose a job or college course that you are interested in. Draw up a series of questions that an employer or a tutor might ask you in an interview for that job or course. Then role play the interviews and make a tape recording of them. Play back the tape recording and discuss how well each of you communicated your answers.

Feedback

Discuss what you consider to be the most important things you have learned about how to prepare a CV and how to prepare for an interview.

6

Choosing Your Future: Options at 16+

What are the options?

You have probably already started thinking about what you will do next year. There are several options, but sometimes it can be difficult to decide which option might be right for you. What seems perfect for one student might not be so suitable for another. People with identical aims don't necessarily have to follow the same route to reach their goals.

Investigate all the options. If you have already made up your mind about what you would like to do and how you will get there, it might still be worthwhile to look at the alternatives. You never know – you might have missed something that would suit you better.

The government has recently introduced a new post-16 curriculum. As a result of these changes students now have a wider range of options from which to choose. Because these changes are so recent, there is still a bit of confusion surrounding all the choices available and where they might lead. This means that it is important that you try to find out the latest facts from a teacher or careers adviser before deciding anything.

There are lots of people who can give you advice on what might be the best option for you. Teachers especially are aware of your strengths and weaknesses.

Qualifications route map

Type of work
Semi-skilled work under supervision/other training

Qualifications needed
4 GCSE grades D–G
GNVQ Foundation (usually 1 year)
NVQ 1

To continue onwards, check out options and any obstacles

Type of work
Skilled work (Foundation Modern Apprenticeships)

Qualifications needed
4/5 GCSE grades A–C
GNVQ Intermediate/ BTEC First (usually 1 year)
NVQ 2

To continue onwards, check out options and any obstacles

Type of work
Technical and supervisory work (Advanced Modern Apprenticeships)

Qualifications needed
AS levels/A2 levels (usually 2 years in total)
Vocational A levels (or AVCEs)/BTEC National (usually 2 years)
NVQ 3

To continue onwards, check out options and any obstacles

Type of work
Professional work
Higher technician
Managerial work

Qualifications needed
Degree
Higher National Diploma – HND NVQ 4/5

What are your choices?

General education courses

(continuing with full-time education at school, sixth-form college or further education college)

▶ GCSEs and GCSE retakes (choices might be limited/unavailable in some institutions)

▶ AS/A2 levels

▶ A levels

▶ International Baccalaureate

Vocational courses

(choices might be limited/unavailable in some institutions)

▶ GNVQs/AVCEs/ BTECs – courses related to a broad area of work, e.g. health and social care, leisure and tourism (different entry levels available)

▶ NVQs – courses related to a particular job/area of work, e.g. Business Administration, Retail; NVQs available at levels 1–5

▶ Or a combination of general education and vocational courses

Training or employment

▶ Foundation Modern Apprenticeships – work plus opportunity to gain NVQ qualification at level 2

▶ Advanced Modern Apprenticeships – work plus opportunity to gain NVQ qualification at level 3

▶ Other training – usually short periods of work experience plus opportunity to gain qualifications

▶ Full-time employment

Post-16 qualifications explained

AS levels and A2 levels

- AS levels (Advanced subsidiary levels) and A2 levels have replaced the traditional A levels. They are designed to be more flexible than A levels.

- AS levels are a qualification in their own right. You cannot take A2 levels until you have first studied the subject at AS level.

- In the first year, students can choose a number of AS levels in different subjects. In the second year, you may continue with the same subjects by taking A2 levels, or start new subjects by taking more AS levels, or start a different course altogether (such as a GNVQ or Vocational A level).

- You will need a minimum of four or five A–C grades at GCSE to get on to an AS level course.

- After AS levels and A levels, you could get a job or go on to higher education. Four AS levels in Year 12, followed by three A2 levels in Year 13, will probably be acceptable by most institutions.

GNVQs and Vocational A levels (or AVCEs)

- GNVQs (General National Vocational Qualifications) and Vocational A levels (sometimes referred to as AVCEs) are vocational courses – they teach you about and prepare you for a broad career area.

- GNVQs are available in schools, sixth forms and FE colleges.

- They can be obtained in a number of ways – by project work, presentations, short tests and exams.

- Work experience placements can be built into the course.

- GNVQs are made up of a number of compulsory units and some optional units, and are offered at Foundation and Intermediate level.

- Vocational A levels (or AVCEs) have replaced Advanced level GNVQs. A double award is roughly equal to two A levels.

BTECs

- BTECs are similar to GNVQ qualifications. Both often cover the same broad career areas, although the exact content may be different.

- BTECs are generally available only at FE colleges.

- They are available at two levels: BTEC Firsts (equivalent to Intermediate GNVQs) and BTEC Nationals (equivalent to Vocational A levels).

- Each level can be taken part-time (as BTEC certificates) or full-time (as BTEC Diplomas).

GCSE Retakes

- Retakes usually take one year.

- Some sixth forms and colleges only offer retakes in English and maths.

- One-year re-take courses usually involve re-sitting two or three GCSEs, and taking two or three new subjects.

- Most colleges and sixth forms will only accept you for re-takes if you have already got D or E grades in a number of your GCSEs.

Key skills

- A new key skills qualification will be offered covering Communication, Application of Number and Information Technology, which can be taken alongside AS levels, A2 levels, Vocational A levels or GNVQ courses.

International Baccalaureate

- This is an international qualification recognised in many countries and accepted in the UK as an equivalent to AS/A levels.

- Students take six subjects, three to four at the higher level. Subjects are chosen from six groups – English, a modern language, humanities/economics/IT, sciences, maths and one other.

- The course includes an extended essay, theory of knowledge and a community service/personal development activity.

Modern Apprenticeships

- Usually lasting for 3 years, Modern Apprenticeships allow students to train on the job so that they can start a career and get qualified at the same time.

- They are designed for students aged between 16 and 18, and are available in over 80 sectors of industry and commerce.

- There are two levels – Foundation (same level as GNVQ level 2) and Advanced (same level as GNVQ level 3).

- A Modern Apprenticeship can lead to university study.

Degrees and HNDs

- Degrees and HNDs are higher education courses. They are usually provided by universities and colleges of further education.

- The most common types of degree are Bachelor of Arts (BA) and Bachelor of Science (BSc), although there are other degrees, such as Law (LLB) and Engineering (BEng). Degree courses take three or more years.

- To get onto a degree course you will have to meet the requirements set by individual colleges and universities. These requirements are usually at least five GCSE passes at A–C level, plus further education qualifications such as A/AS levels and Vocational A levels. People can get onto degree courses following different routes, such as taking an Access course or an HND.

- HNDs tend to be more vocational than degrees and often have a practical element to them. For example, you can get an HND in subjects like Business, Accounting and Tourism. Courses take two or more years.

- As with degree courses, the college or university offering the HND will set the course entry requirements. You will usually need GCSEs and further education qualifications such as A/AS levels, Vocational A levels and/or GNVQs.

Discrete courses

- Many further education colleges offer courses designed for students who need extra support. Discrete courses tend to have smaller groups.

- Subjects available are likely to include art and design, computer skills and reading and writing.

- If you have particular learning/support needs, you should make the college aware of this when you apply.

Considering the options

How important are qualifications?

Three 16-year-old London boys talk about the choices they made and why.

Terry Coventry, *centre*

'Education is important because without it you won't do well in life. But I don't go to school and I haven't done any GCSEs or A-levels. I used to work at the market but I got the sack so I'm looking for a job at the moment. I do worry about the future because I don't want to end up like a bum, so I know it's important to get a job and save money.'

Scott Bland, *left*

'You don't need any qualifications these days. I've done my GCSEs and I've already had loads of jobs. That's without doing my A-levels. I'm working in a printing company at the moment but I don't know what I want to do when I'm older yet. I left school because I hated it, not because I wasn't any good at it.'

Lee Brigati, *right*

'I've done my GCSEs and I'm doing my A-levels at the moment. It's good to have qualifications behind you. But I do think as long as you've got ambitions in life you can do anything you want. If you want it you should go for it. The girls around here are staying in education longer than the boys. They like it more.'

In groups

1. Discuss the views of the three 16-year-olds.
2. How important do you think it is to have qualifications?
3. Lee says that more girls are staying in education in the area where he lives. Is this true of your area? If so, why do think more girls than boys stay in education?

Role play

Role play a scene in which someone tries to persuade a 16-year-old who says that they are fed up with school and education, and that they want to leave and get a job, that they should either stay on at school or go to college because it's vital these days to get qualifications.

for your folder Write a statement expressing your views on how important you think it is to stay on in education and get qualifications.

Considering further education

When choosing your course you need to think about:

- Whether you prefer coursework and continuous assessment or exam-based study.
- The actual syllabus that is covered in either AS/A2 level, GNVQ, Vocational A level or BTEC courses.
- Your GCSE grades and predicted future success. (Speak to school GCSE teachers.)
- Whether your GCSE 'profile' is broad and strong enough for your chosen course of study.
- Your future career plans.
- Whether you would like to mix and match courses and qualifications to suit your strengths and interests.

Which school/college?

When you have decided on what type of course, the next question is where to study. You may be very settled in your present school, but if your school does not have a sixth form, or does not offer the course you want, you may have to change.

If this is the case, do your research:

- Collect sixth form and college prospectuses.
- Go to open days.
- Talk to staff and students.
- Check your journey and travel costs.
- Think about the type of environment – is it right for you?

Adapted from *Action 16* 2001, Prospects Careers Service

What about quality?

A number of schools and colleges may offer similar courses. It's a good idea to check on the quality of the courses on offer. The success of past students is usually a good indicator. All schools and colleges have to publish information about exam results. This is collected each year.

Considering training and employment

When considering these options you will need to think about:

- What future opportunities could develop.
- The skills you will acquire.
- The kind of work you may want to do in the future, and how the training/employment you choose will enable you to achieve your ambitions.
- What support/supervision is available - opportunities for reviewing your progress and opportunities for development.
- What you can find out about the trainer's or employer's previous experience with school leavers.
- How you will cope financially.
- What you feel about continuing to live at home if finances make other choices impossible.

In pairs

1. Discuss all the possible sources of help and information available. Who are the best people to help you make a choice about your further education?
2. Discuss the advantages and disadvantages of the options available.
3. Discuss the advantages and disadvantages of staying on at your present school for post-16 courses and of moving to a college. Give reasons for your views.

What about a gap year?

Some students decide not to go straight to college or university after school. Instead, they opt for what is known as a gap year. In fact the term is a bit misleading, because the best gap years are not simply an escape from 'real' life but ways of learning new things – perhaps within a different culture – and of enabling you to face your chosen career option with a new set of skills and more confidence in your ability to handle just about anything life throws at you.

Away from familiar surroundings and people you know, you have to rely on your own resources. Facing up to loneliness can be a growth point and you sometimes find out that you are capable of more than you thought. Travel may be an important part of the year's experiences and this in itself can be a real challenge, as can learning to adapt to different customs, beliefs and ways of life.

How to start planning

- Talk to your parent(s) or carer about your idea – you will need their support.
- Talk to your teachers about how they think you would cope, about the options available and about implications for college/university applications.
- If possible, find someone who had a gap year and ask them to be honest with you about the pros and cons.
- If you are thinking of travelling, start by doing some serious research on the countries you are considering – use libraries, bookshops, embassies and the web (e.g. TheSite.org has some information on researching a year off).
- If you are thinking of working for at least some of the year, think through the areas which connect to your chosen career path.
- Consider the financial implications.

Reviewing your progress and development

From time to time, it's good to review your progress and development. Why? For a start, it can help you clarify your aims in life and the things you want to achieve. Secondly, it can give you a clearer picture of what you need to do or the changes you need to make to fulfil your potential or achieve your goals. Thirdly, you may be surprised by how much you have changed and by some of the things you have achieved. Recognising these things can be very good for your self-esteem and your self-confidence.

One good way of reviewing your progress is to draw up a personal statement, such as the one on page 35.

Compiling a personal statement

A personal statement needs to cover all areas of your life. As well as reviewing your academic progress, you will need to consider the skills you have acquired and how you have grown and changed as a person. You should think about out of school and extracurricular activities, work experience, community service schemes and what you have learned through your relationships as well as what you have learned through your progress in lessons.

You might also wish to include some reflection on any difficulties you have overcome or any problems you have solved. These areas of your life can also provide evidence of your development and growth. Sometimes you learn more from overcoming a difficulty successfully than you do from achieving something which comes easily.

 On your own

Think about the following questions.

- What piece of academic work, coursework or project work were you most pleased with and why?
- What difficulties have you faced in your school work this year? How have you sorted out your problems?
- What particular aspect of your progress in school do you feel most pleased about? (This might be in academic work, or in sport or in a responsibility you have carried out within school or in your relationships…)
- What goals did you set for yourself last year? How far have you got in achieving these?
- What has helped/hindered you most in progressing towards your goals?
- What new things have you learned and what new skills have you acquired this year?
- Who has been the best personal support to you during this past year?

Make notes on all of these questions under clear separate headings.

 **In pairs**

Discuss your lists of notes. Talk about anything you may have omitted.

 On your own

1. Write up a draft statement, based on the notes you have made. It's a good idea to do this on a computer because that means it is much easier to make alterations and additions later.

2. Arrange an appointment with your tutor and discuss your prepared statement with him/her.

3. Go back to your draft statement and make revisions and changes according to the advice given to you by your tutor.

   - Make sure that your statement is well organised and clearly expressed.
   - Think carefully about layout, font size and style.
   - Check your text carefully before you print it out.
   - Hand the statement to your tutor who will then sign it to show that it is a true statement of your achievements and progress.
   - File the finished statement along with all your other school documents and records.
   - Make sure you have a back-up on disk.

PERSONAL STATEMENT

During Years 10 and 11 I have been studying history, German, geography, art and media studies, as well as the compulsory subjects of maths, English and science.

Although I do not dislike any of my subjects, I particularly enjoy those which involve writing, like English and history. I am fairly successful at both of these. I enjoy doing coursework. I've learned how to work under pressure and I'm much better at keeping to deadlines than I used to be.

My favourite subject is history. I enjoy finding out about the past and linking that to what is going on in the world today. Doing small, individual research projects is something I am quite good at and enjoy, but I also work well under close supervision.

I am prepared to take the lead and will carry out tasks to the best of my ability. If I am asked to do something, I can be relied on to do it without supervision. I am capable of thinking for myself and making sensible decisions. When carrying out a task I can adapt my way of thinking to fit the problem rather than always having to follow the same processes.

I think that I'm good at working with other people. At first, during the year, I found it difficult when other people weren't cooperative. But I've become more assertive now and have developed my negotiating skills.

Throughout my school career I have always maintained a good standard of dress, wearing the correct uniform, and I have always been punctual.

During my time at secondary school I have taken part in several extracurricular activities. I have been in the school swimming team and have been involved in two school drama productions – one as a prompter and the other as a general stage assistant.

I think that becoming a school prefect this year has been very beneficial. My duties as a prefect have included a number of after-school activities, including two open evenings and an induction day for future Year 7 students.

I have also participated in a sponsored 12-hour sports day to raise money for a local school for disabled children.

In Year 10 I did a work placement with a local charitable organisation, which I found extremely interesting and useful as I learned a lot about fundraising and the day-to-day running of a registered charity. I have applied for a place at sixth-form college next year and I am looking forward to starting A-level study.

Signature (Student) ....

Signature (Teacher/Tutor) ....

Date ....

Media images and eating disorders

There is a lot of pressure from the media for young people to be thin. But is it healthy?

Thin stars on TV 'put pressure on the young'

Images encourage women to try for the impossible, says BMA

The abnormal thinness of women on television and in magazines may be putting so much pressure on young women that it is contributing to eating disorders, carrying a high death rate, say the British Medical Association.

The image of the female form being projected in the media was so unrealistic that it encouraged vulnerable young women to try for the impossible, it warned.

But extreme skinniness – particularly as demonstrated by some fashion models – was 'both unachievable and biologically inappropriate', the association said in a new report.

'Young girls try to emulate the very thin women they see on television and in adverts, and it's not possible without starving themselves. Even if they don't die they can cause themselves permanent irreversible damage,' said a BMA spokesman.

Research has estimated that most fashion models and television actresses in the nineties had 10 to 15 per cent body fat – as opposed to 22 to 26 per cent for a healthy woman.

The gap between the media ideal and reality appears to be making eating disorders worse. The result is that women are pressurised, feeling their bodies are fat by comparison, and vulnerable adolescents are particularly susceptible. Low self-esteem is part of the reason for the development of eating disorders, which have complex causes.

Adapted from a report by Sandra Barwick in *The Daily Telegraph*

60,000 suffer eating disorders

Around 60,000 people in Britain suffer from eating disorders. The majority are young women, but one in 10 is male.

Anorexia nervosa affects one to two per cent of women aged between 15 and 30. Of those, between six and 10 in every 100 patients dies as a result of the disorder.

Research shows that girls with low self-esteem at ages 11 to 12 are at greater risk of developing severe signs of eating disorders and wider psychological problems by the time they reach 15 to 17. It has been estimated that 95 per cent of women diet at some time, compared to a quarter of men.

But men still account for 10 per cent of eating disorder sufferers, with many finding it difficult to seek help.

From the *Daily Express*

Fashion chief defends use of skinny models

Fashion bosses' obsession with 'superwaifs' such as Kate Moss was condemned by doctors yesterday for fuelling eating disorders which can kill young women.

'Female models are becoming thinner at a time when women are becoming heavier, and the gap between the ideal body shape and reality is wider than ever,' said a British Medical Association report.

But last night a top modelling agency hit back, arguing the emphasis on slim women merely reflected rather than determined the public's appetite.

The Premier modelling agency, which represents Naomi Campbell and Claudia Schiffer, said women who bought fashion magazines featuring thin models were as much to blame as the editors and advertisers who used them.

'It is very difficult to pinpoint exactly who is responsible,' a spokesman said. 'It is a supply and demand thing – advertisers, magazines and agencies supply the image that consumers want to see.

'Statistics have repeatedly shown that if you stick a beautiful skinny girl on the cover of a magazine you sell more copies. Women go and buy these magazines – Vogue, Cosmo, Just Seventeen. Agencies would say we supply the women the advertisers want. The clients would say that they are selling a product and responding to consumer demand. At the end of the day it is a business and the fact is that these models sell the products.'

Adapted from an article by David Smith and Kirsty Walker in the *Daily Express*

We **must** change our ideal of beauty

Dr Phil Hammond

From the *Daily Express*

The BMA's stance on this issue should be welcomed but, unfortunately, it is not going to change attitudes on its own. Society needs to change its entire view on what it finds attractive.

We all have to change our views or young women are going to carry on missing out on vital nutrients by skipping meals and smoking to keep their body weight down.

We must remember that it is not just women who are affected by slimming diseases. Like female actresses and models, the image of the waif-like man is currently very popular and muscles are out.

The problem is that it is very hard to prove that high-profile people and models are responsible for this growing wave of eating disorders. Doctors do not get young women coming to see them who say they want to look like Calista Flockhart.

These advertising and catwalk images are very subliminal and we are bombarded with pictures of lollipop women every day.

On one Polynesian island, researchers found that the number of women with eating disorders increased dramatically after Western culture invaded the island. I think this is the most convincing evidence the two are related.

Models – what do you think?

 In groups

'I try to like myself for what I am but I open a magazine and immediately compare myself with those perfect models.'

(Jacqueline, 17)

'Everywhere I look there are skinny people, which makes me hate myself even more. I wish magazines would stop portraying "fat" as being bad.'

(Amy, 16)

'Sometimes I wish supermodels didn't exist and body shape didn't matter because then you wouldn't have to keep up.'

(Anonymous, 16)

'Why can't we have healthy role models of all sizes, so it's fair to everyone? Why does everyone have this Beauty Thing? It's like a curse and eventually wrecks people's lives.'

(Kelly, 14)

1. Discuss these views and the views expressed by Eileen Ford and the spokesman for the modelling agency (page 36). Are people obsessed with being thin because of the fashion industry and how supermodels are portrayed in the media?

2. 'We must change our ideal of beauty.' Do you agree with Dr Hammond? If so, how do you think people's attitudes to beauty could be changed?

Positive or negative?

Models do not have a negative impact on women. They have a positive impact because they set standards. Women are going to look like themselves but they will look their best selves because models set standards. When you think you look your best and feel your best, there's an aura around you of self-confidence and self-assurance. Models do that to women.

– Eileen Ford, US model agent

 **Feedback**

Share your views on the effect of media images of thinness in a class discussion.

Crash dieting can damage your health

Millions of people go on diets, many because they are influenced by society's message that if they can 'only shed those extra few kilogrammes', they will be more attractive, sexy, popular and successful. Although there is nothing wrong with sensible diets, problems begin when they get out of hand. Dieting can develop into anorexia, although there are other factors present. The obsession with losing weight is linked to bulimia and compulsive eating. Diets can work if they are controlled and gradual, but many crash diets and wonder diets can be extremely unsafe.

David's story

David was overweight, and he decided to go on a crash diet. He bought special 'meal-replacement' drinks from his chemist. Instead of eating a meal, he would have one of these drinks. Each drink contained 110 calories, giving him a daily intake of 330 calories. David formerly had been used to eating 5000 calories or more.

Although he lost weight very quickly, he started having headaches and feeling nauseous and dizzy. He was extremely miserable, but he continued with the diet.

Eventually David decided to seek medical treatment for his headaches.

According to his doctor, the headaches were a direct result of the diet.

The number of calories David was taking was far too small for his body. He was weak and unable to concentrate because he was simply not eating enough food. David's doctor gave him a much more sensible diet which meant he lost weight more slowly but more safely.

The lack of calories affected David's blood chemistry and blood sugar levels. Before long he would have become dehydrated and constipated. Over a period of time, the body starves and starts to nourish itself on muscle. The heart is a muscle, and it is extremely dangerous if that is devoured in the body's attempts to continue all its functions. It will become weakened, and can be damaged to the point that it can cause the person to have a fatal heart attack.

From Eating Disorders by Kate Haycock

The **right** amount of the **right** foods

Experts agree that the best way to stay the right weight for your height is to eat a healthy, balanced diet all the time. That means a mixture of foods containing all the nutrients which the body needs. People who eat a healthy, balanced diet when they are young are less likely to have weight problems when they are older. They set a pattern of eating which they can follow all their life.

From Eating Disorders by Jenny Bryan

Diets turn 'normal eaters' into people who are afraid of food. Food takes on all the punishing and magical qualities that anguish the compulsive eater. Our cultural obsession with slimness creates a whole new grouping of women who are unnecessarily drawn into having a food problem. As the women attempt to get slimmer, the diet organisations get fatter and fatter on their pain.

From Fat is a Feminist Issue by Susie Orbach

In groups

1. Does dieting help people with a weight problem or just encourage them to continue their unhealthy eating pattern?

2. What is the best way to deal with a weight problem?

For research

What types of foods contain the nutrients you need to keep healthy? Find out how much of each type of food a 15-year-old boy and a 15-year-old girl needs and what is a healthy, balanced diet for a teenager.

Don't Be Conned – *Learn to Like the Way You Are*

Two advice columnists say what they think about dieting and the pressure on people to get thin.

Annabel Goldstaub says ...

If you would dearly love to be thin but aren't, ask yourself why. It's easy to believe that if you were slimmer your life would change instantly. But waiting to be thin in order to find the perfect job, pass your exams, take care of your appearance or find yourself a boyfriend is just a waste of time.

The diet industry is big business. In the UK it is worth over £1 billion annually.

Relax a bit ... Take a permanent break from strict dieting. It never served in making you happy anyway, did it? If you're truly worried about your shape and eating habits talk it out with a sympathetic friend or go and see your doctor.

Learn to be happy with yourself the way you are and don't let society pressurise you into being a shape that isn't right for *you*.

From Just Seventeen

Anita Naik says ...

It's hard not to agonise over your body when every time you turn on the TV, open a magazine, or watch a film, there are images of skinny women with extra long legs, perfect breasts and shiny hair wandering in front of your eyes. And it's hard not to become obsessed with what you eat when everyone from your mother to your friend seems to be on a diet.

The fact is there is a huge diet culture in the Western world aimed specifically at women. We're made to feel conscious of our bodies from an early age and encouraged to watch what we eat, because if we're not slim then we're supposedly not attractive. Yet we're not all born to look like supermodels. We all come in different shapes and sizes, with different hip measurements and different body weights. Not all of us have to have 'manageable, shiny hair' that bounces when we walk. Or clear perfect skin that 'glows with health'.

A 'normal' woman has hair that doesn't go right some mornings, gets spots when she's stressed out and stuffs her face with chocolate when she wants to. She is a real person, not some advertisement for a 'perfect' woman. No one is ever 100% happy with the way they look but as long as you feel about 80% happy then you're on the right track. If you think you're scoring about 20% then it's time to reassess your attitude to yourself.

Having a good body image is important because it makes up a vital part of our self-confidence and esteem. If you don't like yourself, you can't expect anyone else to like you back. Learning to respect yourself, warts and all, is a way of saying, 'Hey, look! I'm a good person. I'm worth knowing.' You don't have to make excuses for yourself or what you look like. You are who you are, and if people can't accept you for that, then that's their loss not yours.

From Am I Normal? by Anita Naik

In groups

1. Discuss the advice given by Anita Naik and Annabel Goldstaub.
2. 'Looks aren't everything. It's what sort of person you are that matters. The most attractive people are those who are positive and happy and, therefore, fun to be with.' Discuss this view.

For your folder Write a short statement expressing your views on supermodels, the fashion industry and the diet culture.

In pairs

Read Sonia's letter to Alice (right). What advice would you give Sonia? Draft Alice's reply.

Dear Alice

I am very worried about my friend. For a while now, she has been behaving oddly as far as eating is concerned. She used to have a good appetite – don't get me wrong, she wasn't greedy or anything, it's just that now she never seems to eat anything and when she's out with us she's always fussing about what's in everything and how many calories it's got in it.

She was on a diet for a while and she looked great. Now she's getting thinner and thinner and is obsessed with exercising. Last week, when we were eating lunch she threw most of hers away! Then in the afternoon, she fainted in Physics. It's just not like her. What should I do? Please help!

Sonia

> "Do you want a sure way to lose weight – one that doesn't require super will-power or lunches of apples and Diet Coke? One that is fun, gives you energy, makes you feel better, and builds your self-confidence? One that keeps your weight down forever and allows you to eat more of the food you like?
>
> There is such a magic formula, and it's called EXERCISE. "

Dr Linda Ojeda, *I Looked in the Mirror and Screamed*

Why exercise?

Statistics show that as a nation we are getting fatter simply because we don't take enough exercise. The latest government research shows young people in particular are ruining their future health, by watching more TV, doing sedentary activities like playing computer games, and being driven to school instead of walking. The simple correlation between an inactive lifestyle like this and weight is simply that the less you move, the more you'll weigh and the less fit you'll be.

Time and again, studies have shown that there is nothing better for you than regular exercise. Twenty minutes, three times a week is all we're talking here. This will not only increase your fitness levels but also decrease stress, keep depression away, prevent sleeplessness and increase your all-round energy levels. To achieve this kind of fitness you do not have to run, go to step classes or invest in dumbbells and fancy trainers. But you do have to do an aerobic and anaerobic activity at a certain intensity to get the physical benefits you need.

Aerobic exercise

Aerobic exercise is exercise which requires a lot of oxygen. Do it regularly and you will:

- Be more energetic, less tired and leaner.
- Have a stronger heart, so it doesn't need to pump as often to pump blood through your body.
- Burn body fat as fuel. This is great if you want to lose weight because body fat will be burnt off and your lean muscle tissue (the stuff that's lost when you crash diet) will stay.
- Reduce your risk of a serious illness and heart disease.
- Increase your metabolism, which means you'll burn off more body fat.
- Increase your endorphin levels. Endorphins are the body's natural painkillers and help to keep you feeling good.

Best aerobic activities

WALKING – This improves cardiovascular strength (the way your lungs and heart work) and muscle strength.

SWIMMING – This improves upper and lower body muscles as well as aerobic strength.

CYCLING – High quality, aerobic exercise that works arms and legs.

Anaerobic exercise

Anaerobic exercise is exercise that uses muscle strength rather than oxygen. Anaerobic exercise, or strength training, is good for fitness because it strengthens your bones and tones and shapes your body. It helps you to build up muscles and shapes your body. It helps you build up muscles that will continue to burn calories even when you're not doing anything. Most people assume you have to lift weights for anaerobic exercise, yet virtually every exercise that uses aerobic energy also uses anaerobic energy.

Do it regularly and you will:

- Feel stronger.
- Burn more calories.
- Have better muscle tone.
- Increase muscle mass which will keep your body healthy.
- Reduce body fat.
- Control blood pressure.

Best anaerobic activities

Any exercise which increases your muscle strength. This can be any kind of work with weights, swimming, tennis, and/or power walking, where you pump your arms as you walk.

Adapted from *Wise Guides – Eating* by Anita Naik

Types of exercise

> *I started on an indoor bike but it was so boring.*
> *Now I go out in all weathers and cycle near my home.*

It's important to choose a form of exercise that you enjoy, that suits you and fits in with your lifestyle. It's pointless, say, to take up jogging in the early morning if you know you loathe getting up earlier than you have to. So you have to decide – do you like sport and playing games with other people? Or do you prefer to do something on your own, in your own time? It's up to you.

If you don't want to take exercise in a formal setting you can still get in shape. You could incorporate a walk into your daily routine; try walking to school instead of catching the bus. Walk fairly briskly but not jerkily and keep up a continuous easy pace. If it's too far to walk, use your bicycle if you've got one.

Running is good for your heart and lungs, and it will also keep you toned up. You'll need to set aside a time each day to run, and wear the appropriate running shoes that provide support and are geared to the type of terrain you'll be running over. Swimming is also an ideal all-round exercise.

From *Every Girl's Lifeguide* by Dr Miriam Stoppard

Role play

'Why does everyone make such a fuss about exercise? If you can lose weight by dieting surely that's all you need to do?' *(Anna, 15)*

Role play a scene in which a friend of Anna's explains to her the benefits of exercise and tries to persuade her that it's better to exercise than to diet.

In pairs

'Exercise is for fitness freaks. I'm no good at games and I hate exercise. I don't see the point of it.' *(Darren, 15)*

Do you sympathise with Darren's point of view? Why? How would you try to persuade him that exercise is important for him?

Looking at lifestyles

Dianne, aged 16

Dianne has just started to work for her A levels at the local college. She doesn't know many people, so she is finding it very difficult. She's also noticed that since leaving school she has put on weight and is feeling unfit. She used to be in the school netball and tennis teams, but they don't seem to play those games at college. She has decided that she needs to lose some weight, so she is not eating breakfast and lunch.

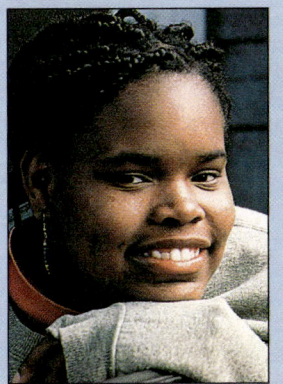

Michael, aged 14

Michael is overweight. His parents run a restaurant and he is allowed to eat what he wants. Because his parents are very busy, he doesn't see them very much. He gets bored in the evening, so he watches a lot of videos or plays computer games. People have started to bully him at school, so he keeps telling his mum that he is ill so that he can stay at home.

Paul, aged 17

Paul has just started working in the local sheet metal factory. He is really enjoying work, and has made a lot of friends who are all in their early 20s. They have started to go down to the local playing fields after work to have a game of football. After playing, they tend to go to the pub for two or three pints of beer. Because of this, Paul is missing his evening meal and making do with nuts and crisps. Most of the people at work smoke, and Paul is wondering whether he should start to smoke too.

In groups

Look at the lifestyles of the people in the case histories above. Identify any unhealthy habits and write down what you think they should do to lead healthier lifestyles.

For research

Between 15 and 20 per cent of middle-aged people in Europe and 1 in 3 Americans suffer from obesity. Research the health problems that result from obesity. Either report your findings in a class discussion or in a short article entitled 'Obesity – a growing problem'.

Feedback

Share your views on the importance of exercise in a class discussion.

From *Health and Fitness in Focus* by Hilary Tunnicliffe

What is Pre-Menstrual Syndrome?

Dr Miriam Stoppard explains:

PMS amounts, in many girls, to a great deal more than simply irritability, depression and a tendency to become tearful. It is a collection of symptoms that varies from girl to girl, but for many, a number of the following symptoms occur regularly in the week before their periods:

- Headaches
- Arthritic pains
- Allergic symptoms
- Inability to concentrate
- Impatience and a quick temper
- A sense that the world is against you
- Physical clumsiness
- Inability to string words together or find a word
- Depression
- Sudden weight gain and bloating
- Insomnia

What causes PMS?

The cause of PMS is extremely complex: several organs and hormones are involved. Almost certainly, the hormone that causes water retention is produced in a higher quantity at this time and that is why diuretics (drugs that cause the body to eliminate water) sometimes help if bloating is the main symptom. In about half the girls who get depressed, there is a relative, and only relative, shortage of vitamin B6. This is why supplements of this vitamin can help depression. You should never take B6 supplements, however, without first seeing your doctor, because unsupervised medication can lead to very serious side-effects.

It is thought that PMS is probably caused by an imbalance of oestrogen- or progesterone-stimulating hormones from the brain, and some girls have this problem because they are short of progesterone. If this happens to you, replacement progesterone therapy can help to relieve your symptoms.

From Every Girl's Lifeguide by Dr Miriam Stoppard

How do you know if you've got PMS?

If you feel you could be experiencing mood swings and/or depression, or physical symptoms such as bloatedness, severe headaches, sore breasts, fluid retention or fatigue, then the best thing to do is to keep a sort of diary of your moods and feelings. This will help you to pinpoint the days you feel bad and link them to when your period starts and ends. Try to keep this diary for at least three months, and if you begin to notice a pattern then it's time to act to beat PMS!

How can PMS be treated?

There is no one single treatment that works for everyone who suffers from PMS. The first thing to do is to consult your doctor, who will probably suggest you try a special diet. Doctors have discovered that eating small portions of starchy foods every three hours helps a lot, no matter what the time of the month. Recommended foods contain flour, rice, oats, potato, maize or rye; so menus including pasta, bread, baked potatoes or corn on the cob will do the trick. You may also find that eating at least four portions of fruit or veg every day can help. It is also important that you eat within one hour of waking up and one hour of going to bed at night. Dividing your meals into six or seven healthy snacks may seem strange when you're used to eating breakfast, lunch and dinner, but this method really can work and is worth trying.

If the diet doesn't work, then your doctor may prescribe some hormone supplements as well.

Adapted from It Happened to Me by Lesley Johnston

for your folder

Dear Erica

Some weeks my fourteen-year-old sister is very moody and irritable and snaps at me all the time. At other times we get on really well and have a great laugh together. My gran says she's probably suffering from PMS. What does that mean? Is there anything my sister can do about it?

Sam

Study the information on these pages, then write a reply to Sam, explaining what Pre-Menstrual Syndrome is, how it can affect girls' lives and what they can do to relieve the symptoms.

Julia's Story

I was 13 when my periods started and the problems came almost right away. I started to get so ratty and irritable that I would cry at almost anything. I was convinced everyone hated me and was paranoid that even my friends were against me.

I also became convinced that I was really fat, ugly and horrible and no one was ever going to want to go out with me because I was so awful. Of course I always got spots before my period too.

People thought I was a bit weird and moody, but I'd be laughing and joking a couple of weeks later like I didn't have a care in the world. One day I would be crying in the classroom and the next I'd be asking if anyone had a tampon, and it began to click there might be a link there.

I think Mum always had an inkling that my periods were bad, so she decided to keep a closer eye on me.

She started to keep a sort of diary of all my symptoms, and after only a couple of months she noticed that everything seemed to be worse for me (both mentally and physically) in the couple of weeks before my period started.

She sent for some information about PMS and I agreed to try the diet outlined in one of the leaflets, which meant I would be eating a starchy snack every three hours or so instead of the usual breakfast, lunch and dinner.

The diet made a difference immediately. Everything seemed to be easier, and suddenly my period would be over for another month and I'd still be in a good mood. The change was unbelievable, and other people noticed too.

Adapted from *It Happened to Me* by Lesley Johnston

How to Beat Your Period Blues

Problem: Getting emotional

Reason: At this time of the month you are on an emotional roller coaster because the levels of hormones in your body are rising and falling. This could mean anything from being on top of the world to feeling like you can't go on.

Solution: Cut junk food, caffeine and sugar out of your diet and switch to mineral water instead of fizzy drinks. Then think about following the starchy 'snack' type of meals outlined on page 42.

Problem: Bloatedness

Reason: Your body tends to retain water when your period is due, so you may get a shock when you try on your tightest jeans, and your breasts may feel swollen and tender.

Solution: Cut salt out of your diet. If you need more help ask your GP about diuretic pills, which help stop water retention.

Problem: Spots

Reason: It's those hormones again! Your skin tends to get slightly more greasy before your period starts.

Solution: Make sure you keep your skin scrupulously clean at all times of the month, and *don't pick* because it could spread infection.

Problem: Anger

Reason: Just as some girls get depressed and despondent, others find they easily lose their temper; changing hormone levels are, again, to blame.

Solution: Try the tips (on page 42) on how to beat PMS and don't be ashamed of explaining what the problem is to other people. Your parents, mates and boyfriend can learn to look for those PMS signs and know when not to wind you up!

Problem: Food cravings

Reason: Your blood sugar levels may be falling before your period, so cravings are your body's way of making sure you take in the food necessary for your metabolism to stay steady.

Solution: Try a piece of fruit rather than a bar of chocolate! The healthier the food you eat is, the more chance you have of combating pre-menstrual problems without resorting to medicines.

Problem: Stomach cramps

Reason: Your womb contracts in order to help dispel the matter shed every time you have a period.

Solution: Try walking about a bit, or some gentle stretching exercises; or it may feel better to have a long bath or place a hot water bottle on your stomach. Some yoga positions can help. If none of these solutions work, try a painkiller.

Problem: Back pain

Reason: The womb isn't right at the front of your body, like you might think. Sometimes contractions or period pain may feel closer to the small of your back than your stomach.

Solution: As for stomach cramps, but try sitting up with a hot water bottle tucked into the small of your back.

Problem: Lethargy

Reason: The depressive symptoms of PMS may make you flake out, or it **could** be because you're having to cope with aches and pains while getting on with your life.

Solution: You'll probably find that a bit of exercise will help when you're having period pain too, and could also sort out those stomach cramps when your period arrives.

Adapted from *It Happened to Me* by Lesley Johnston

Look after your skin

ACNE

Nearly every teenager has acne at some stage. During adolescence high levels of sex hormones are secreted, which lead to the production of large quantities of sebum in the skin. Sebum is an irritant that may block the pores causing a purplish lump, which may become infected and form a pustule. One or two pimples are only to be expected but severe acne tends to scar, so ask your doctor for an acne preparation to help clear it. There are many good ones, but you'll need a prescription.

From *Every Girl's Lifeguide* by Dr Miriam Stoppard

Acne – Your Questions Answered

Q. My spots seem to get worse just before my period. Why is this? – *Catherine, Sussex*

A. Many women find that their acne is more noticeable at this time. Doctors do not know why this happens, but it may be related to changes in hormone levels during the menstrual cycle.

Q. I love eating chocolate. But will it bring me out in spots? – *Tony, Cardiff*

A. In some people, chocolate and other fatty foods might encourage acne. If that seems to happen, then cut it out! But for most sufferers, diet is not a factor. In general, however, it is a good idea to aim for a balanced diet, with plenty of fresh fruit and vegetables.

Q. I have quite a few spots on my face. How often should I wash? – *Jane, Manchester*

A. It is a good idea to wash your face twice a day with normal soap and water. If you have both dry and greasy areas, use a non-greasy moisturiser on the dry areas. Many people believe that acne is caused by dirt or poor hygiene, but this is not the case.

Q. I just cannot resist squeezing my blackheads. Will I end up with scars? – *Trevor, Edinburgh*

A. Almost certainly! If you squeeze blackheads or spots, you may force the contents deeper into the skin rather than onto the surface. This could lead to cysts and scars later on.

From an article by Peter Moore in *Guardian Education*

66 Acne made me feel miserable

I had no confidence at all and went round with hunched shoulders, not daring to look people in the eye. In shops and on public transport I always felt people were looking at me and I developed the habit of staring at the floor.

The worst thing about my acne was the constant advice people gave me on how to clear it up. The lads at school suggested I eat less chocolate, and my mum's friends told me to drink lots of water. I knew they were trying to help so I was polite, but inside I was infuriated because I was already eating a healthy diet and drinking eight glasses of water a day. Their advice seemed to imply it was *my* fault I had spots.

At school I tried to avoid bullies by keeping a low profile, sitting at the back of the class and not saying much during lessons, but I was still called 'spotty' and other nicknames more times than I care to remember.

One day the drama teacher decided I was to play Romeo in the school play. Romeo is supposed to be this handsome hero and I thought everyone would laugh at me. I tried desperately to get out of it, but the teacher insisted I play the part. In the end I did get comments, but it wasn't as bad as I'd imagined.

I'd say to anyone else suffering from acne, yes, try to get it sorted out, but looks aren't everything – you can still be a nice person and enjoy life without a perfect complexion. 99

From Mizz © Simone Cave/MIZZ/IPC Syndicaton

Jason, an ex-acne sufferer

In pairs

Study the information on this page and produce a Test Yourself quiz consisting of ten statements about acne, some of which are true and some of which are false. For example, 'Acne is an infection caused by a virus. True or False?' Then give your quiz to another pair for them to do.

Feedback

Share what you have learned about acne in a class discussion. Talk about how people who have acne feel and what effect teasing them about it can have on them.

Stay *Safe* in the *Sun*

All ultraviolet rays in sunlight – both UVA and UVB – are harmful to the skin, and the damage depends on the length of time you stay unprotected in the sun. Long exposure to the sun may inflame your skin and cause it to swell. Even longer exposure results in burning, with blistering and peeling, and possibly heatstroke, which causes the temperature-regulating mechanism of your body to give up, making you very ill.

The most serious danger of suntanning is the risk of skin cancer, which is very high in pale-skinned Northern Europeans. Skin cancer has increased by 40 per cent in the last few years and this is almost entirely attributable to our obsession with a tan. Sunblocks are the order of the day.

Another long-term hazard is wrinkles, which are caused by the sun destroying the collagen in the skin. A suntan ages your skin and there is nothing you can do to reverse it. Instead, protect your skin with sun cream in strong sunshine. Always wear a peaked cap or broad brimmed hat and a protective top. If you really must get a tan, learn all about sun protection factors (see below).

Why use a suntan cream?

Suntan creams block the harmful effects of UVA and UVB light. You'll find each cream comes with a sun protection factor (SPF), which equates to the length of time you can stay in the sun without burning.

So if you're sitting in strong sun that would give you sunburn in ten minutes and you apply a suntan cream with an SPF of 10, you can sit in the sun for 10 x 10 minutes without burning. Very pale-skinned people should use creams with the highest SPF or a total sunblock.

From Every Girl's Lifeguide by Dr Miriam Stoppard

Role play

In pairs act out a scene in which a teenager argues with one of their parents who is trying to persuade them to put on some suntan cream before sunbathing.

Tattoos

Some people decide to have their skin tattooed. But you need to think carefully before you get a tattoo. Lots of people get a tattoo on the spur of the moment, then live to regret it.

Tattoos are fast becoming an essential accessory for pop stars and showbiz personalities. Mel B (Scary Spice), Mel C (Sporty Spice) and Robbie Williams are just three examples of tattooed pop singers who have encouraged a craze for tattooing among their fans.

In groups

1. Why do people have tattoos done? Would you ever consider having a tattoo?
2. Why is it risky to tattoo yourself or to let a non-professional tattoo you?
3. Why do many people who have themselves tattooed eventually regret it?
4. What do you think of people who have tattoos?

for your folder 'I wish I'd never had it done.' Write a story about a person who got themselves tattooed, then regretted it.

Body piercing

Body piercing has become increasingly fashionable in recent years. Some people choose not only to get their ears pierced, but other parts of their bodies, such as their eyebrows, nose and tongue as well. It's vital if you choose to get any part of your body pierced that the person doing it uses properly sterilised equipment. Reusing unsterilised equipment could lead to the spread of infections such as hepatitis or even HIV.

If you are thinking of getting a tattoo...

▲ **Make sure you go to a licensed tattoo parlour, where you know the needles will be clean.** One of the most common ways of contracting AIDS is from dirty needles.

▲ **Do NOT attempt to do it yourself, or ask your mates to tattoo you.** Not only is there a health risk, but you may regret the result.

▲ **Remember that it is far cheaper to get a tattoo than to have one removed.** Tattoos can be removed by laser treatment, but it's very unlikely you'll be able to do so unless you pay for the treatment yourself.

In groups

Discuss what you think of body piercing.

Teenagers under pressure

Stressed out !!!!!!!!!!!!!!!!!!!!!

Teenage stress is a real problem but it can be beaten, just don't suffer in silence, says Victoria Stanley

It gets to us all sometimes. That anxious, gloomy feeling called stress. It can make the most minor problem (what *am* I going to wear to that party?) feel like a matter of life and death and the prospect of a big event such as an exam seem like the end of the world.

OK, so stress blows problems out of perspective. But that doesn't mean you have to put up with it.

For many teenagers stress starts at school. 'I just have to hear the word "exam" and I begin to panic,' says 16-year-old Joanne from Telford. 'I feel sick … like I want to give up when all I want is to do well. And there's always a new story in the paper about someone with a string of A grades to torment me.'

There's also the pressure of large workloads, long days, bullying at school and just wanting to be liked.

At home there might be family problems – from arguing with your parents to dealing with a divorce. Then there's the 'bigger picture', with young people more likely to worry about environment, crime and unemployment problems.

'I feel there are so many expectations to live up to'

'I'm a typical teenager – bored unless I'm doing something out-of-the-ordinary,' says Joanne. 'I get stressed by being "stuck in the middle" and not knowing if I'm coming or going. I also feel there are so many expectations to live up to and that if you're not rich, famous or successful then you don't stand a chance.'

But despite the big pressures Joanne feels, she also admits stress can come from something as simple as being tired. If you've ever had one too many late nights and ended up in tears over 'nothing' you'll know what she means.

Just as there are many causes for stress, the way it shows itself also changes. Stress can make you feel like you don't want to be around other people. It can turn you off your food or make you binge, stop you sleeping properly and even be the reason for stomach pains, backache or a stiff neck. Irrational fears are also common. That's when one bad mark makes you think that you're a total failure.

But for all the negative effects, stress can actually be good for you. A small amount can give you the buzz or adrenaline rush you need to perform. Too little stress can result in boredom and feeling frustrated with life. The key is balance and learning how to beat off unhelpful levels of anxiety.

It's good to know that, according to Gavin Ward of the Health Education Authority, many of us use stress-busters. 'We do things to beat stress every day without knowing it,' he explains. 'Going to your room and sticking the music on really loud, heading out for a kick around or just chatting to a friend on the phone can all do the trick.'

Regular exercise, a good diet and activities like dancing can even stop you getting stressed in the first place.

Whatever you do, dealing with stress is vital. The highs of being a teenager – the freedom, the excitement of trying new things, the possibilities that lie ahead of you – are wrapped up with the lows. As Joanne knows, 'Problems will come up all through life but I think you have to experience the downs to appreciate the good bits.'

From an article by Victoria Stanley in *The Daily Telegraph*

The signs of stress

Physical signs of stress	Mental signs of stress
Headaches	Irritability
Chest pains	Bad temper
High blood pressure	Depression
Insomnia	Inability to concentrate
Eczema	Overreacting to problems
Asthma	Inability to relax
Palpitations	Intolerance of noise
Tiredness	Impulsive behaviour
Dandruff	Feeling panicky

From *Health and Fitness in Focus* by Hilary Tunnicliffe

What stresses you out?

Stressful situations
for students

- Lack of privacy
- Concern about appearance, weight or identity
- Conflict with parents
- Difficulty in making decisions
- General feelings of frustration
- Death of a parent
- In trouble with the law
- Concern about choosing a career
- Handling sexual relationships
- Loss of a parent through divorce
- Not being part of the in-crowd
- Death of a close friend
- Serious health problems, e.g. surgery
- School pressures, exams, deadlines
- Recent move of home, school or college
- Parents having rows or in financial trouble
- Break up with boy- or girlfriend
- Money troubles
- Death of a close relative

From an article by Victoria Stanley in T2, *The Daily Telegraph*

League table of what stresses you out

The top causes of adult stress are bereavement, divorce and moving house. Students from a Chelmsford Girls' School and a London boys' college listed their top five causes of stress for teenagers.

Boys

1. **pressure to be macho**: trying to be tough and physically mature
2. **image**: coolness of clothes, pressure to look good, acne
3. **girls**: looking good and acting cool in front of them
4. **class-mates**: bullies, lack of self-confidence, peer pressure
5. **competition**: exams, sport and just about everything else

Girls

1. **exams**: coursework and homework
2. **parents**: imposing restrictions on going out/boyfriends
3. **friendships**: arguments and problems
4. **peer pressure**: what to wear/look like
5. **being organised**: demands made on ability to be so

In groups

1. On your own study the list of stressful situations for students (above). Rank them in order of importance, starting with the most stressful. Then compare your rankings with those of other people in your group.

2. Discuss the findings reported in the 'League table of what stresses you out'. Do you agree that boys and girls get stressed out about different things?

Seven Ways of Beating Stress

1. **Think positive** If you feel awful, remember that you won't feel that way forever. Things move on and time changes the way we feel about how serious problems are.

2. **Learn to relax** Take up meditation, learn visualisation or buy a relaxation tape. Herbal teas and aromatherapy oils can also help you to chill out.

3. **Be creative** It's a great way of de-stressing. Scribble, paint, draw or try pottery. Writing a diary can help express how you feel.

4. **Take time for yourself** Listen to music (really loud), read a mag, have a relaxing bath, have a kick around … whatever works for you.

5. **See friends** This is a great way to deal with your problems. They can give you support and advice or simply be there for you.

6. **Get active** Make time for a favourite sport or activity. Exercise can turn anxiety into positive energy.

7. **Talk about it** Sharing your worries makes a huge difference. It could be a friend, teacher or family member you can trust. Or call a confidential helpline

From an article by Victoria Stanley in T2, *The Daily Telegraph*

Don't waste time worrying

I used to be a huge worrier – everything was a drama. I would worry about stupid things like being late, not wearing the right clothes or being cold-shouldered by my mates. Then my mum had a long talk with me. She said, 'What's the point in worrying about the future. If the worst happens then you'll have worried twice. If the best happens you'll have worried for nothing.' Mum was right. Worrying is a waste of time.

Paula, 17

In groups

Discuss the seven ways that are suggested for beating stress (above). Which do you think are the two most helpful tips?

Feedback

Discuss what you have learned from these two pages about what causes teenagers to feel stressed, what the signs of stress are and how to deal with stress.

for your folder

Everyone has stressful experiences. Thinking about how other people have coped with stress can help you to understand how to cope with your own problems.

Write about someone you know who has experienced a lot of stress. Who or what helped them to cope? What can you learn from their experiences? Write one or two paragraphs on this topic.

What depression is

There must be few people who always feel good about themselves and are completely satisfied with their lives. Most people like themselves in some ways and not others, and like some aspects of their lives but not others. They may sometimes go through bad patches but do not think of themselves as having mental health problems. For others life is more of a struggle. They feel bad about themselves and their lives in most ways. At times they feel complete despair. It is this last group who can be said to be depressed.

From Understanding Depression, MIND

What causes depression?

There is no one single cause of depression. It can be brought on in many different ways, for example by the feelings of loss when someone close to you dies.

Having strong negative emotions – guilt, fear, anger and grief – all these can lead to a person feeling depressed.

What else can cause the blues?

Any change can trigger a bout of depression – parents' divorce, remarriage of a parent, moving house or changing schools, break-up with a best friend or with a boy- or girlfriend.

Failure of some sort can also make you feel down. For example, not doing well enough on big, important exams, or not winning a hoped for scholarship.

Inability to make friends easily can lead to loneliness and the feeling of being left out. A step beyond this is being deliberately ignored by schoolmates, gossiped about, or even bullied.

Depression can also have physical causes, too. Being ill for a considerable time can leave you feeling very down. A bout of depression can follow a bad dose of 'flu, probably because the body – especially the immune system – is tired.

Poor diet, lack of physical fitness and drug abuse can also contribute to depression. Food allergies can also cause depression. Certain foods affect people adversely – gluten, for example, found mainly in wheat, oats, barley and rye, can be responsible for depression in someone even mildly allergic to it.

Adapted from Bad Hair Day by Nancy Scott-Cameron

66 What does it feel like to be severely depressed?

Last year, when I was 14, everything and everyone seemed to be getting at me. I would shut myself away in the loos at school and cry because I hated it so much. I couldn't cope with my work, and a teacher had told me that if I was going to do well in my GCSEs then I needed to pull myself together. She didn't realise that when I got home at night I just stared at my books and crawled into bed instead of tackling the stuff I couldn't get the hang of. Inside I was so tired and the easiest option was to shut it all out. I felt like it was pointless to try working because I would never understand anyway.

Things were bad at home too because my parents spent a lot of the time fighting. I would sometimes sit in the park till 10 p.m. rather than face going back after school. I got more and more introverted, and whereas I used to tell my mum when I was feeling low, now I would ignore her. – *Rebecca* 99

From It Happened to Me by Lesley Johnston

How do I know if I have serious depression?

Of course, you'll know you're sad and not your usual self. But here is a list of other symptoms:

- ☐ Feeling lonely and isolated.
- ☐ Feeling trapped in a situation – no way out.
- ☐ Being moody and irritable – even violent.
- ☐ Losing interest in everything – school, family, friends, hobbies, sports, and personal appearance.
- ☐ Feeling it almost impossible to make the simplest decision, such as what clothes to wear.
- ☐ Eating too much or too little.
- ☐ Feeling no sense of self-worth.
- ☐ Finding difficulty in sleeping, perhaps waking very early in the morning, or just the opposite – sleeping too much.
- ☐ Finding difficulty in concentrating. Often all symptoms are worst in the morning, and depressed people find it extremely hard to rouse themselves out of bed.
- ☐ Having thoughts of running away, self-harm or suicide.

From Bad Hair Day by Nancy Scott-Cameron

⊕ In groups

Discuss what you have learnt from this page about what depression is, what causes it, what it feels like to be depressed and what the symptoms of depression are.

Dealing
with
depression

Most people feel depressed once in a while. You may not have experienced it before, but when you do you may feel like the whole world is falling down around you. There are lots of things which can trigger off depression; perhaps it's school or your friends, or even your parents. But ultimately, most people get depressed because they dwell too much on the bad things that happen to them. No doubt every person alive would sink into a pit of despair if they counted all the things that had gone wrong in their lives. So if you're feeling really depressed, try thinking of all the positive things that have happened to you and cross out all those minuses you've built up.

There's nothing wrong with being depressed every now and then – no one can expect to be happy all the time. But if you do feel your depression is getting out of hand, then there are people, like your doctor, a teacher or any other person you can trust. Having someone to talk to can really help when you're down. It doesn't have to be someone you know well, sometimes just a voice at the other end of a phone can be comforting.

If you find that you really can't bring yourself to talk to anyone, then try writing down your problem on a piece of paper. Underneath the problem, list all the possible solutions to it. You'll be surprised at how this simple exercise can be really helpful. The most important thing to remember is that you are not alone … help is at hand.

From *Just Seventeen*

'I want to kill myself'

Suicide is never an option. Apart from destroying your life it will also destroy the lives of those closest to you. There is NO problem that can't be worked out – as long as you ask for help. If you feel at all suicidal please don't give up on life, as there are a number of places and people that can and will help you come to terms with the pressure you're under. Both the Samaritans and Childline are on hand 24 hours a day, 365 days a year, and your GP can also refer you on to someone who can help. Talking through your problems with someone who understands is more helpful than you think. All worries are all things that can be worked through. They are not things to throw your life away over. Whatever you do, don't suffer alone. Seek help now.
– *Anita Naik.*

From *Am I Normal?* by Anita Naik

If you feel like *running away …*

Erica Stewart lists some dos and don'ts for those of you who may feel like leaving home when you get depressed.

DON'T assume that your problems will magically disappear as soon as your home is left behind. OK, you're feeling desperate, but you've still got somewhere to live. You're far better off trying to sort out what's bothering you before doing anything rash.

DO remember there is always somebody you can talk to about how you feel. You can get confidential advice and they won't tell your family you've spoken to them if you don't want them to.

DON'T think that running away will automatically make you feel better. At the end of the day, whatever caused you to feel depressed will be unresolved, and you'll probably feel even more depressed without your home comforts.

DO try talking to your family and letting them know how low you feel and what's bugging you. You may be surprised at just how sympathetic they are and how much they can help.

DON'T think that nobody will miss you and care about your being gone. However convinced you are that they won't, I can assure you they will.

In pairs

Who do you think is the best person to confide in and ask for help if you are very depressed – a relative, a friend, your doctor, a teacher, a social worker, someone from your place of worship, a person from a helpline such as the Samaritans?

Role play

In pairs, act out a scene in which a teenager asks an adult how to help another teenager who has told them that they are feeling very depressed.

For research

Use the library and the internet to do further research on depression among teenagers and how to deal with it. Then use the information, together with what you have learned from these pages, to produce a leaflet for people of your own age describing what depression is, how to identify whether you're severely depressed and offering advice on how to deal with depression.

Safer Sex

Taking responsibility

Safer sex is about many things – not having sex at all, avoiding intercourse when you do have sex, or using contraceptives (especially condoms) to protect yourself from unwanted pregnancy and from infection. Above all it is about being assertive, knowing what you want and talking and negotiating with your partner.

> Poor skills in talking about sex, negotiating relationships and taking responsibility for the outcomes may be a significant factor in the UK's high rates of teenage pregnancy. Interestingly, one study found that a far higher proportion of Dutch boys – two and a half times as many as their British peers – discuss contraception with their partners before sex. The rate of teenage births in the UK is six times that in the Netherlands.

Adapted from *Teenage Pregnancy*, report by the Social Exclusion Unit

In groups

Read the quote above and the extract 'Talking about sex', then discuss the following questions.

1. Why do the writers stress the importance of talking about sex?

2. Do you feel uncomfortable talking about sex, either with your friends, your parents or your partner? Why is this? What would make you feel more comfortable talking about sex?

3. Do you agree that young men find it more difficult than young women to talk about their feelings? Is this healthy? What can we do about it?

4. How could talking about sex allow both partners to get 'more of what they want'?

5. How could talking about sex 'save our lives'?

6. When is the right time to talk about contraception with a partner?

Talking about sex

66 But they just get in the way! Just when you're getting down to some real action, you're not gonna stop and say – Excuse me, I must put my condom on now, if you don't mind. **99**

It seems that, for most young people – and especially young men – sex is something you do, not something you talk about. If you don't know something, then you act as if you do. In order to be able to take responsibility for contraception, young people have to learn to become more comfortable talking about sex (and they must be encouraged to find out the facts when there is a gap in their knowledge).

Talking about sex means talking about how you feel, and again, this is not something young men are encouraged to do. To complicate things further, sex is supposed to be 'spontaneous' – it just happens, and, once the process is started, it is somehow unstoppable. 'Taking responsibility' is usually seen as something negative, especially by young men.

This needs to be reframed. Without talking, safer sex practices become very difficult. Talking about sex could help save our lives. But, put more positively, talking can be presented as a way of both partners getting more of what they want – no unwanted parenthood, no hurt or angry partner, no upset family and a better and more relaxed, safer, more fulfilled sex life. What more could you want?

Adapted from Boys Will Be...? Sex Education and Young Men, by Neil Davidson

Taking responsibility for condoms

> Young women often carry condoms but do not want to produce them for fear of seeming calculating or promiscuous. Many young men don't like them, and many women lack the confidence to insist on using them. Generally, many young people seem to regard contraception as more 'taboo' than sex.

Adapted from *Teenage Pregnancy*, report by the Social Exclusion Unit

In groups

1. Why are young men and women reluctant to use condoms? Is this a sensible approach to sex?

2. Should young people carry condoms? If so, who should take responsibility to carry them? Discuss the views of the young people (below).

> 'I don't carry condoms. I don't think that's my responsibility. It's up to the boy to decide whether or not to use them.'

> 'If a girl starts carrying condoms everyone thinks she's a slag.'

> 'If you think you might have intercourse, it's common sense to carry condoms, rather than to rely on your partner having some.'

> 'It's ridiculous to suggest everyone should carry condoms. It suggests everyone's promiscuous and that all teenagers are having sex, when in fact lots of them are being sensible and waiting till they're older.'

Saying **no** to sex?

Minimising the risks from having sex means planning, being careful about what you actually do with another person and making sure you do not do things that you do not wish to. This is what safer sex is all about.

It is not a good idea to be involved in sexual activity until you are sure that you want to. Some people suggest that young people should be encouraged to say no to sex and remain celibate. In America, this has led to campaigns to get young people to make a 'virginity pledge' and say they will not have sex until they are married. Other people regard this as unrealistic.

From *Sex Matters* by Julian Cohen

 In groups

1. 'You should wait until you're married before you have sex.' What do you think? Should young people be encouraged to make a 'virginity pledge'?

2. If a teenager is being pressurised by their partner to have sex but does not want to do so, what should they say and do?

Teenagers regret having sex too early

Early sexual experience is more likely to be associated with regret. The younger the age at first intercourse, the higher the percentage who feel they had sex too soon. However, there are marked gender differences. More than half of women (58.5 per cent) for whom first intercourse occurred before the age of 16 judged this to have been too soon, but less than a quarter of men did (24.4 per cent). Qualitative surveys have suggested that young men are more likely to perceive their first sexual experience as positive than young women. This may be due to different expectations of the experience, or a 'rites of passage' effect for young men.

A survey of 13 to 16 year olds in London, Birmingham and Newcastle areas found that sexual experiences were regretted due to:
- the influence of drink or drugs (43 per cent boys, 9 per cent girls);
- it happening in the heat of the moment (33 per cent and 40 per cent);
- they thought it would be different (16 per cent and 20 per cent);
- they felt pressured (8 per cent and 31 per cent).

From *Young People's Sexual Attitudes and Behaviour*, Sex Education Forum

> There's lots of pressure on girls to have sex to prove they're not 'drags' and on boys to have sex to prove that they're 'macho'. But to have sex just for the sake of what other people will think is a ridiculous reason. The sensible and responsible thing to do is to wait until you feel it's the right time for you and your partner. And if that means waiting until you're older, that's the mature thing to do.

Erica Stewart

I'm concerned about contraception

I'm 15 and I've been going out with my boyfriend for three months. I want to start having sex with him but I don't know what to do about contraception. Should I ask to go on the pill and should he wear a condom? I'm worried about getting pregnant and I don't want to catch an STI. I need your help because I can't talk to anyone about this, especially not my boyfriend. I'd be too embarrassed.

Erica Stewart says:

I'm really worried by your letter. You say you want to start a sexual relationship, but you're too embarrassed to talk to your boyfriend about what's worrying you. If the two of you aren't close enough for you to talk about your concerns and to discuss what contraception to use, then it seems to me you don't have the sort of relationship you need to have before you start having sex.

Choosing what contraception to use should be a joint decision. One of the main reasons why I think the age of consent should be kept at 16 is because I see too many underage girls like you rushing into having sex when they haven't developed the necessary emotional closeness with their partner.

But if you're determined to start a sexual relationship, then my advice is to go on the pill and to use a condom. You can get full information about these from your local family planning clinic.

 **In groups**

1. Discuss the reasons why young people say they regret having sex too early (left). What different reasons do boys and girls give? Do the results of the survey surprise you?

2. What pressures are there on teenagers to have sex? Discuss Erica Stewart's comment (below, left) and say why you agree or disagree with it.

In pairs

Discuss the following letter to a magazine's agony aunt and draft a reply to it.

Dear Erica

My girlfriend and I have been going out for nearly a year and I want to have sex with her. She keeps on saying she wants to wait. We get on really well, but it's starting to be a thing between us. How can I convince her to give in?

Preventing an unwanted pregnancy: contraception

Contraception

If young people choose to have intercourse, there are ways they can protect themselves from unwanted pregnancy. While there are many different forms of contraception, none are ideal. Perhaps the most effective methods for young people are to use both the female pill and male condoms.

The pill can be obtained through family doctors, family planning clinics and agencies such as Brook. It is free and can be prescribed to under 16s without parental consent if the young girl is sufficiently mature and does not want her parents to know. Effective use of the pill involves understanding how it works, taking it regularly and having regular medical check ups. Although it is very effective in preventing pregnancy it does not protect against STIs and HIV.

The coil (intrauterine device or IUD) is rarely given to young women because of the risk of pelvic infections, which can lead to infertility. The **diaphragm** (or cap), **sponge** and **female condom** can all be difficult to place properly in the vagina and can be a bit messy. They tend to be used by women who are more experienced with sex and confident enough about their bodies to use them properly.

Natural (or **rhythm**) **methods** involve avoiding intercourse at times when a woman is most fertile. The woman has to keep a chart of her periods and carefully plan when to have intercourse and when to avoid it. Even done properly it is not a very reliable method.

Injections like Depo-Provera or Noristerat can provide up to three months' protection but are not usually recommended for younger women. In America, Norplant is the latest contraceptive used by young people. Small rods containing a chemical contraceptive are put into the girl's arm. Norplant can provide up to five years of protection, but it can have unpleasant side effects.

Condoms are an effective form of contraception if used correctly; they also protect against STIs and HIV (see below) – something that none of the other forms of contraceptive do. They are essential for heterosexual couples who have vaginal or anal intercourse and gay men who have anal intercourse. Stronger condoms are recommended for anal intercourse. Condoms can be bought from chemists and vending machines but can also be obtained free from family planning clinics. They need to be used carefully if they are to be effective.

Emergency contraception

If a woman has unprotected intercourse and thinks she could become pregnant she can do something about it as long as she acts quickly. Emergency contraception (the 'morning after' pill) can be obtained from doctors and family planning clinics. If taken within 72 hours (three days) of unprotected intercourse, emergency contraception can ensure the woman does not become pregnant.

Adapted from *Sex Matters* by Julian Cohen

 In groups

1. Why is it important to use contraception when having sex?
2. What are the advantages and disadvantages of the different forms of contraception listed in the article above?

Preventing sexually transmitted infections: safer sex

Each year more than 1 in 20 adolescents contracts a curable STI. Sexually transmitted infections are among the most common causes of illness in the world.

World Health Organisation

Safer sex and safe sex

During sexual contact infections can be passed from one person to another. These are known as sexually transmitted infections (STIs) or sexually transmitted diseases; see page 53 for further information on STIs. Anyone who is having sex can get a sexually transmitted infection from an infected partner if they do not use any protection.

Safer sex

Safer sex means sex that reduces the risk of infection. The best form of protection against contracting an STI is to use a condom during sexual intercourse. Using a condom is not absolutely safe, however, as condoms can break. They are also only effective if they are used correctly.

Oral sex (one person kissing, licking or sucking the sexual areas of another person) does carry some risk of infection. If a person sucks the penis of an infected man, for example, infected fluid could get into the mouth. The virus could then get into the blood if you have bleeding gums or tiny sores somewhere in the mouth. The same is true if infected sexual fluids from a woman get into the mouth of her partner. But infection from oral sex alone seems to be very rare.

Safe sex

Safe sex means sex which is absolutely safe. Lots of activities are completely safe. You can kiss, cuddle, massage and rub each other's bodies. But if you have any cuts or sores on your hands make sure they are covered with plasters (band-aids).

SEXUALLY TRANSMITTED INFECTIONS

Sexually transmitted infections (STIs), or sexually transmitted diseases, are infections passed from one person to another during sexual contact.

TYPES OF SEXUALLY TRANSMITTED INFECTIONS

There are many types of sexually transmitted infections:

Common
- Genital warts
- Chlamydia
- Non-specific urethritis (NSU)
- Genital herpes
- Gonorrhoea (the clap)

Less common
- Trichomonas vaginalis (VG)
- Syphilis (the pox)
- HIV (Human Immunodeficiency Virus)
- Hepatitis B and C
- Infestations, including scabies and pubic lice (crabs).

Some of these infections are very serious. For example, HIV is the virus which causes AIDS (see page 54). Hepatitis B can cause liver problems such as cirrhosis (scarring) or liver cancer. Syphilis can cause permanent damage to the heart, brain and nervous system if left untreated.

Other infections are occasionally, but not always, spread through sexual contact. These include thrush, bacterial vaginosis and cystitis.

HOW DO I KNOW IF I HAVE A SEXUALLY TRANSMITTED INFECTION?

People who have a sexually transmitted infection sometimes get symptoms to show that something is wrong. But often they don't.

Some warning signs to look for:
- An unusually thick or watery, cloudy or smelly discharge from the vagina (not to be confused with the normal slight discharge which all women have).
- A discharge from the penis.
- Itching, rashes, sores, blisters or pain in the genital area.
- A pain or burning sensation when you pass urine.
- Urinating more than usual.
- Pain during sex.

But remember:
- Sometimes there are no symptoms.
- Symptoms may not appear for months.
- Symptoms may disappear when there is still infection.
- You can have more than one sexually transmitted infection at a time.

Untreated sexually transmitted infections can cause serious and permanent damage. Get yourself checked out straight away if you have any of the symptoms listed above or if you think your current or a recent partner has an infection.

Go to your own GP or any NHS sexual health clinic, often called STD (sexually transmitted disease) or GUM (genito-urinary medicine) clinic (see page 55). You can find details of your nearest NHS sexual health clinic in the phone book.

Some facts about STIs

- Many sexually transmitted infections have no obvious symptoms of illness, so you could have an infection and not know it.
- Sexually transmitted infections occur frequently in both men and women.
- Many sexually transmitted infections are curable and all are preventable.
- Delaying treatment could mean that the infection gets worse and other problems could occur.
- A mother can pass on an untreated infection to her child during pregnancy and birth.

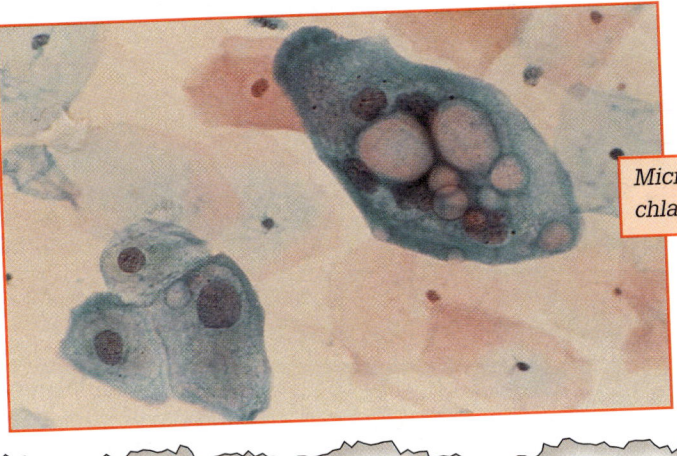

Microscopic view of the sexually transmitted infection chlamydia (pink spheres inside blue cell, top right)

Adapted from *Sexually Transmitted Infections*, Health Education Authority

In pairs

1. Study the information on these pages. What are the ten most important things you have learned about STIs? Make a poster – 'Ten key things you need to know about STIs'.

2. Draft a reply to this letter to a teenage magazine's agony aunt:

> I've been having sex with my boyfriend for a couple of months. We've been using condoms but he tells me he hates them and that none of his friends bother with them. He says it'll be alright because he'll withdraw before he ejaculates, so I won't get pregnant and I won't catch anything. He knows he hasn't got any infection because he hasn't got any symptoms. What should I do?
>
> Tania, 16

HIV, AIDS and Sex

What is AIDS?

AIDS is short for Acquired Immune Deficiency Syndrome. It is a serious condition in which the body's defences against some illnesses are broken down. People with AIDS develop many different kinds of disease which the body would usually fight off quite easily.

What causes AIDS?

There is clear evidence that AIDS is caused by a virus called HIV, which is short for Human Immunodeficiency Virus.

If a person becomes infected with HIV, does that mean they have AIDS?

No. HIV is an unusual virus because a person can be infected with it for many years and yet appear to be perfectly healthy. But the virus gradually multiplies inside the body and eventually destroys the body's ability to fight off illnesses.

It is still not certain that everyone with HIV infection will get AIDS. It seems likely that most people with HIV will develop serious problems with their health. But this may be after many years. A person with HIV may not know they are infected but can pass the virus on to other people.

How could I become infected with HIV?

The two main ways in which a young person can become infected with HIV are:

- By having sexual intercourse with an infected partner.
- By injecting drugs using a needle or syringe which has already been used by someone who is infected.

HIV can be passed on in both ways because the virus is present in the sexual fluids and blood of infected people. If infected blood or sexual fluid gets into your blood, then you will become infected.

If a man with HIV has vaginal intercourse without a condom, infected fluid could pass into the woman's bloodstream through a tiny cut or sore inside her body. This can be so small that you don't know about it. If a couple have anal intercourse the risk of infection is higher than with vaginal intercourse.

If a woman with HIV has sexual intercourse without a condom, HIV could get into the man's blood through a sore patch on his penis or by getting into the tube which runs down the penis.

If there is any contact with blood during sex, this increases the risk of infection. For example, there may be blood in the vagina if intercourse happens during a woman's period. There can also be bleeding during anal intercourse.

'It won't happen to me'

Some people think that AIDS is something that other people need to worry about – gays, drug users, people who sleep around. These ideas are mistaken. All young people, whoever they are, wherever they live, need to take the threat of AIDS seriously.

Your chance of becoming infected depends entirely on how you behave. You can only become infected with HIV if you engage in risky activities. If you have sex without a condom with a number of different sexual partners, or share needles or syringes with several other drug users, you increase your chances of coming into contact with someone already infected.

AIDS has made sex more difficult. It is one more thing to think about. But AIDS is not something to be so frightened of that it puts you off ever having sex. Be clear about the risks, and if you do decide to have a sexual relationship with someone, avoid activities that are risky (see pages 52–53).

Adapted from 'HIV and AIDS information for young people', Avert

In pairs

Design a poster aimed at teenagers: 'How you can reduce the risks of getting infected with HIV.'

For research

Find out more about the AIDS epidemic, how it affects young people worldwide and the progress that is being made in the search for a cure.

Feedback

Organise and video-tape a live TV-style debate on the issues about safer sex raised in this unit. Discuss what can be done to cut the high rate of teenage pregnancies in the UK, how to minimise the risks of catching STIs and why everyone should be concerned about the AIDS epidemic.

'I took a risk and paid the price'

When 16-year-old Gabrielle had unprotected sex she had no idea what ordeal lay ahead of her. She soon discovered she'd a sexually transmitted disease.

Going to the clinic

It took quite a lot of courage to actually go to the STD clinic, but once I got there it wasn't half as bad as I imagined.

When I walked into the waiting room I thought everyone would stare at me, but it wasn't like that at all. I mean, everyone was there for the same reason so no one could judge me! The staff at the clinic know it can get embarrassing and so I didn't even have to give my name – I was given a number!

I really didn't know what the doctors would think of me in the clinic, but they weren't judgmental at all. In fact the nurse I saw was really nice. She started by asking me quite a lot of questions about my past sexual experiences. That was quite embarrassing but I thought, 'Well, there's no point in lying because they'll need all the facts to treat me.'

She then explained that she wanted to do an examination. I had to lie on a bed and put my feet into a pair of stirrup things, then she used a metal, funnel-like object called a speculum to look inside my vagina and took a swab for analysis. Unfortunately, at the time I was so nervous that all my muscles tightened up and the examination hurt a bit which made me really angry with myself for not being able to relax more.

The worst bit was waiting for the results

Anyway, they took quite a few tests, including a blood test and a urine sample and then I had to go back to the waiting room. Some results only took ten minutes to come back and luckily they were all negative. The other results took a week so after the examination was over I went home and waited.

That week was awful because I was really worried about what might be wrong with me and I was coming up to my GCSE exams, which was added pressure. I kept the whole experience secret from my parents but in the end I had to tell someone so I told one of my best friends. When she found out she was great about it and said she'd do anything to help. All I could do then was wait for the results …

Finding out what was wrong with me

When I phoned the clinic for the results the following week they told me that I had chlamydia and I'd have to go back for treatment. I'd never heard of it before, although they told me that it's the most common STD.

Chlamydia's actually very dangerous in women because if it doesn't get treated early, it leads to something called Pelvic Inflammatory Disease (PID). PID can lead to infertility so I was lucky I went to the clinic when I did.

After the doctor explained all this to me I was given some antibiotics and told to come back once I'd finished them to check it had cleared up. I went back to the hospital for my final test when the antibiotics were finished and I was all clear. What a relief!

Be aware of the risks

I felt really stupid about catching an STI, especially through unprotected sex which was really silly of me. But it's not disgusting or dirty – it happens and you should make yourself aware of STIs in case it happens to you. A few of my friends didn't understand what I was talking about when I told them about chlamydia. I think everyone my age should know the risks, because AIDs and pregnancy aren't the only dangers when you have sex without a condom.

From *Mizz* © MIZZ/IPC Syndication

In pairs

Draft a reply to this letter to a teenage magazine's agony aunt.

I'm worried I may have caught something. After the last time I had sex, I had a slight discharge. I don't want to go to my doctor, because someone might see me at the surgery and my parents might get to know. Should I tell my girlfriend? What should I do? Ralf, 16

Having an HIV test

Many people think there is a test for AIDS. In fact there is no test for AIDS. There is a blood test that can detect the antibodies to HIV, the virus that eventually leads to AIDS. If someone 'tests positive' it means that they have the antibodies and also have HIV.

When people feel they have put themselves at risk of contracting HIV through unsafe sexual practices, they may think about whether to have an HIV test.

Some people who feel they have put themselves at risk of getting HIV decide to take the test. Others decide that, even if they may have HIV, it is better not to know. The decision about whether or not to have a test can be very difficult and that is why it is very important that people have counselling beforehand to weigh up the pros and cons and decide what is best for them.

Some people are happier knowing for sure whether or not they have HIV. If they do not know they may worry all the time and find it difficult to get on with their life. Getting a negative result would be a great relief.

Getting a positive result may enable people to start health checks and treatment earlier. Although there is no cure for HIV or AIDS, certain medical treatments may help slow down the progression of HIV to full-blown AIDS. A positive test may also mean they can alter their lifestyle so that it is

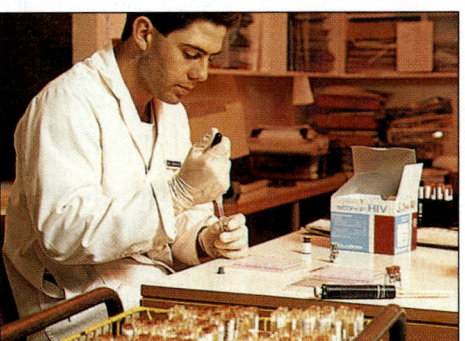

healthier. This can be important because HIV involves a breakdown of the body's immune system, decreasing resistance to common infections.

Adapted from *Sex Matters* by Julian Cohen

In groups

If you think you've put yourself at risk of being infected with HIV should you go for a test? Give reasons for your views.

Teenage Drinking

Alcohol – the facts

It's against the law for teenagers under 18 to buy alcohol, but when they were asked if they had drunk alcohol in the previous week, over 40% of 15-year-olds said 'yes'.

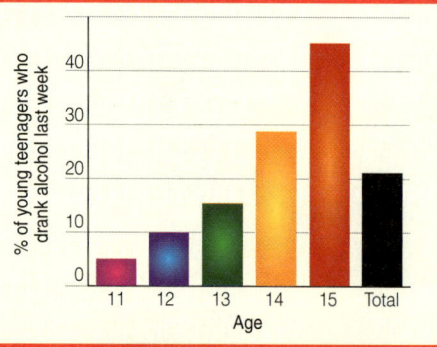

Bar chart: % of young teenagers who drank alcohol last week, by Age (11, 12, 13, 14, 15, Total)

Alcohol
– what are its effects?

If you decide you're going to have an alcoholic drink, it's worth knowing how it's going to affect you.

What is alcohol?
It's an intoxicating depressant drug that after an initial buzz will make you feel down.

How does it affect you?
It acts on the central nervous system slowing down the body and brain. After one or two drinks, most people begin to feel less inhibited and more relaxed. After several drinks, you may begin to slur your speech and become clumsy. More alcohol could result in staggering, double vision, loss of balance, vomiting, 'room spinning' and mood swings (going from high emotion to aggression is not uncommon). This explains the accidents while driving, for instance, fights and making decisions you regret.

How long before drink takes effect?
Five to ten minutes. It can last several hours, depending on …
- how quickly it is drunk, whether there is food in your stomach to soak it up;
- your weight (the smaller you are the less body fluid you have to dilute alcohol – why girls generally get drunk quicker than boys);
- what you drink (fizzy drinks like alcopops hit your brain faster);
- how used to drinking you are (over time the liver learns to break down alcohol faster; this is why it takes very little alcohol to get you drunk at first).

Why the hangover?
Alcohol dehydrates and strips the body of blood sugar. This can lead to a mixture of feeling/being sick, thumping headaches, sweating, nervousness and shaking.

Any other downsides?
Binges (drinking too much in one go) are far more harmful than drinking moderately – drunks choking to death on their own vomit while unconscious is a (rare) worst-case scenario. Sustained and heavy drinking can lead to addiction, liver disease, ulcers, heart problems, accidents and even suicide.

The hard facts

> Drinking alcohol together with taking illegal drugs is particularly dangerous, increasing the likelihood of a serious drug overdose.

> Around half of all pedestrians aged 16-60 killed in road accidents have more booze in their bloodstream than the legal drink-drive limit.

> 1000 children under the age of 15 are admitted to hospital each year with acute alcohol poisoning. All need emergency treatment.

> One in four teenagers, especially boys, get into arguments or fights after drinking alcohol.

> Around half of all adults admitted to hospital with head injuries are drunk.

> Alcohol is a factor in at least 7% of accidental drownings and 40% of household fires.

> You can get a criminal record for offences of drunkenness. Being drunk will be no excuse if you end up in court on a charge of criminal damage or violence.

> In 1994, 57,800 people were found guilty or cautioned for drunkenness. The peak age for offenders was 18.

> About 28,000 deaths a year are linked to alcohol.

Adapted from Alcohol: Facts for Young People, Health Education Authority

In groups

Drinking by young people has increased a lot during the last twenty years. Why do you think this is? Below are some suggestions. Can you think of any others?

- Young people have more money than they used to.
- Young people have followed the example of their elders.
- Because of the stresses of modern life.
- The power of advertising.

Why drink?

> **'If alcohol disappeared, there'd be no way to enjoy yourself.'**
>
> *Mike, aged 17*
>
> We all like a laugh. And you can't have a laugh on a night out if you're not going to have a drink or several, can you? Trouble is – with alcohol there's no off switch if you decide you've had too much.
>
> You're with a group and you're drinking rounds, or maybe sharing a bottle or a six pack. You're drinking quickly, keeping up with your mates.
>
> Before you know it, you're feeling really rough. So you have another drink, hoping you'll feel better. And pretty soon you're not feeling much at all.
>
> Except when you wake up the next day and can't remember how you got there or what you did. **And how scary is that?**

Alcohol: Facts for Young People, Health Education Authority

Reasons for NOT getting completely TRASHED

There are loads of reasons for not getting completely trashed. For starters:

★ You're more likely to make a hit with someone you're keen to impress if you're being yourself.

★ You'll be able to look out for your mates if things get out of hand.

★ You might avoid doing something you'll regret. Like getting off with Mr or Miss personality bypass or having sex when you don't really want to or not bothering to use a condom.

★ No more throwing your guts up all night.

★ You'll get home safely and getting up won't be so bad.

★ You'll feel and look better. Unless your idea of attractive is a blotchy face, bloodshot eyes, a furry tongue and depressed to boot.

★ You'll be fitter. Drinking damages the muscle fibres you need for sport.

★ You won't blow all your cash on an evening out you can't remember.

Alcohol: Facts for Young People, Health Education Authority

So, why do people do it?

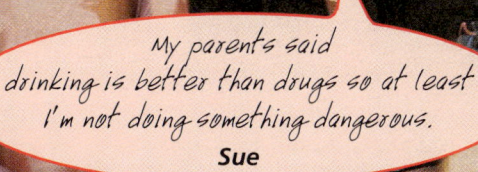

I'm quite shy and need to get into the party spirit.
Lee

Everyone does it. If I didn't everyone would think I was a real square.
Sam

My parents do it all the time and it's never done them any harm.
Paul

My parents said drinking is better than drugs so at least I'm not doing something dangerous.
Sue

I do it because I get bored.
Karen

The first time I got drunk I was 12 – I did it because I wanted to see what it felt like.
Linda

Wise Guides: Drugs by Anita Naik

 In groups

1. Look at the sections 'The hard facts', 'Reasons for not getting completely trashed' and the statements from young people about why they drink. Select the points you think young people need to be most aware of if they decide to drink.

2. Look at the way 'Reasons for not getting completely trashed' is presented. Is it written in an appropriate way for your age group? Why/ why not? Would it have any effect on your behaviour? Give reasons for your views.

3. What would you say in response to each of the young people quoted above?

 **Feedback**

Share your views with the whole class.

How much is too much?

ALCOHOL:
what it is and what it does

All alcoholic drinks contain pure alcohol in varying quantities. The strength of alcoholic drinks is shown by a number which may be preceded by the word 'alcohol' or the abbreviation 'alc', followed by %vol. This is known as the alcohol by volume (abv).

Alcohol can be measured in 'units'. Increasingly drinks are being labelled with the number of units they contain. This can help you work out how much alcohol you drink in a day and compare it with the daily benchmark.

for your folder Design a poster to warn young people about the importance of thinking before drinking.

Daily benchmark guide

5 UNITS
4 UNITS
3 UNITS
2 UNITS
1 UNIT
0 UNITS

Men can drink between 3 and 4 units a day with no significant risks to their health

Women can drink between 2 and 3 units a day with no significant risks to their health

1 unit =

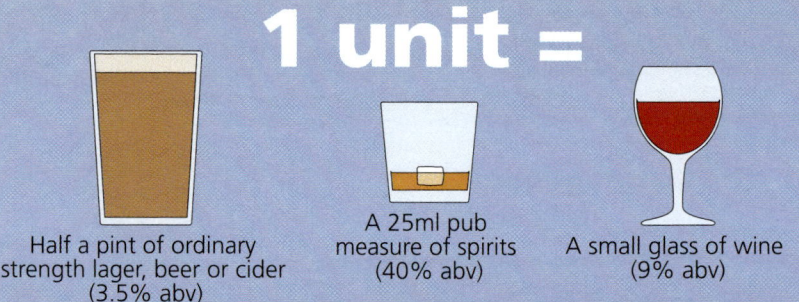

Half a pint of ordinary strength lager, beer or cider (3.5% abv)

A 25ml pub measure of spirits (40% abv)

A small glass of wine (9% abv)

What about alcopops?
Did you know … there can be as much alcohol in a 330ml bottle of alcopop as in a generous shot of whisky.

Have **you** got a problem?

The first thing to consider with alcohol is how much you or your friends actually drink. Most people consider themselves to be sensible drinkers and yet drink way above their weekly unit allowance.

If you are worried about your habits, then start by putting together a drink diary for a month. Include every drink of alcohol you have, and try to note down where it was, how big the glass was and what you actually drank (be honest!). Then note how you felt the next day and how many hangovers you've had. This way you can see if you're way over the limit or drinking sensibly.

Warning signs to look out for in others, or in yourself:

- Being drunk more often than not.
- Skipping school because of a hangover.
- Having accidents because of drinking.
- Becoming touchy when people talk about drinking.
- Lying about how much they drink.
- Needing to have alcohol around.
- Drinking alone.
- Frequently mixing different types of drinks.
- Using drink to get through the day.
- Binge drinking at weekends.
- Becoming irritable and anxious if they can't have a drink.
- Not being able to make it through a night out without having a drink.

The Morning After

Adapted from an article by Jenny Tucker in *Just 17*

A girl lies in bed staring at the wall. She's just woken up and she's feeling terrible. Her head's pounding, her stomach's turning somersaults and the more she recollects of last night, the worse things seem. She went to a party and had far too much to drink. She thinks the evening ended in bed with a boy. Everything's a bit fuzzy so she's not sure, but the worry about whether or not she's pregnant has just begun. If only she hadn't …

Romie Goodchild from the Family Planning Association, who sees many examples of after party pregnancy, says 'Be aware of the dangers *before* you go to a party. Have a good time but also have the courage to say no to alcohol – and sex.' Having said yes to one it's often hard to say *no* to the other, as one of the girls who wrote to us discovered.

> 66 *I'd had a few drinks and I tripped over something in the room and started giggling. The boy said 'I knew you wanted it all along,' and jumped on top of me. I hadn't had sex before but I think he had sex with me. I was frightened and I wonder if I might be pregnant. I'm 14.* 99

This girl was under the age of consent for both intercourse and alcohol. If she did become pregnant the boy could be prosecuted and, because she's so young, heavy drinking is likely to damage her physically. On top of that, this sort of experience could affect her emotionally for the rest of her life.

Getting blind drunk is silly, but it's possible that you don't even realise *what* you're drinking. Some people find it hilariously funny to mix people's drinks or kid them into thinking that a pint of vodka and orange is really a peculiar-tasting mug of squash. When you've crashed into the wall for the fifth time you'll realise that it wasn't.

On top of all that, being totally legless is dangerous, especially with inexperienced drinkers. People die from alcoholic poisoning and if you're not a hardened boozer it only takes the equivalent of three-quarters of a bottle of spirits consumed in less than four hours to be fatal.

You could even end up having sex without *knowing*. How? By getting so plastered that you pass out.

In groups

Talk about the risks involved in getting so drunk that you don't even remember whether or not you've had sex or who you had sex with.

In pairs

Look at the following letters and discuss how you would respond to them. Draft a reply to one of them.

Dear Clare

I'm seriously worried about my friend's drinking habits. Last week a group of us went out for the evening. We were having a laugh and a few drinks but Sam's drinking was way out of order. She got so drunk that she chatted up a complete stranger and ended up accepting a lift home from him. Fortunately nothing happened to her but I'm frightened that she could put herself at risk. What should I do?
– Mike

Dear Anna

My boyfriend is usually really shy and gentle. I say usually because at a party last week I saw a completely different side to him. He got completely drunk and picked a fight with someone over nothing really. I am worried that drinking makes him aggressive and I don't know what to do if he gets drunk again when we are out together.
– Martina

For research

Find out about the work of organisations which help people to overcome alcohol problems.

13 Drugs Issues

Young people and drugs

Lots of young people experiment with drugs. So there may be situations in which other people put pressure on you to take drugs. Whatever they say, all drugtaking involves some risks. Before you make a decision, it's worth knowing as much as you can about drugs and drugtaking.

From *Right Angle*, Save the Children

Drugs factfile

> Up to 40 per cent of young people in the UK have tried drugs by the time they are 16 years old.

> More than one in ten young people are regular users. 14 and 15 year olds are most at risk from hard drugs such as heroin.

> Use of drugs has increased eightfold among 15 year olds and fivefold among 12 year olds in the past ten years.

> People take drugs for many different reasons but they are sold for one reason: profits.

ALL DRUGS CARRY RISKS

- The effects may be unexpected.
- Many drugs sold on the street have been mixed with other substances, so users can never be sure what they are getting.
- Users may become tolerant to some drugs (e.g. alcohol, heroin and speed). This means their bodies have become so used to the drug they need to take more to get the effect they want.
- Users may overdose (take too much for their bodies to handle). With alcohol, heroin, gases, glues and aerosols, an overdose can prove fatal.

From *The Score – Facts about Drugs*, Health Education Authority

Why do young people use drugs?

The reasons why young people use drugs are many and varied. If you just read the tabloid newspapers you might think young people only used drugs because they are bored, pressured by friends or forced to use them by evil drug-pushers. In contrast, people who use drugs often say they get something positive and pleasurable from the experience. To really understand why someone uses drugs you need to take account of what it means to the user. The motivation for using drugs will be different for different people. Reasons for drug use can have a lot to do with how people deal with their emotions. They may use drugs to feel better about themselves, to escape emotional upset, to feel less anxious, to avoid thinking about things or making decisions or to make them feel independent. There may also be more physical reasons such as blocking out physical pain and the pleasure of the 'buzz'. Drugs may also be used to increase or reduce energy levels or to help people relax.

Some motivations for drug use seem to have a lot to do with the users' relationships with other people. Using drugs may help some people feel accepted by others, make them feel less shy and lonely or make communication with people easier.

Other reasons for drug use may have more to do with the environment in which people live. If drugs are freely available and not too expensive the temptation to use will be greater. There may also be pressure from friends (peer pressure). Some people would add that many young people are tricked into drug use by drug dealers who give youngsters free drugs and get them hooked.

From *Life Files: Drugs*

In groups

1. Why do some people start taking drugs? List all the reasons you can think of.

2. How do young people obtain drugs? What is your attitude towards people who sell drugs to young people?

3. What do you consider to be the main risks involved in drugtaking?

What about the law?

The two main laws about drugs are the Medicines Act and the Misuse of Drugs Act. The Medicines Act controls the way medicines are made and supplied. The Misuse of Drugs Act bans the non-medical use of certain drugs.

The Misuse of Drugs Act places banned drugs in different classes – A, B and C. The penalties for offences involving a drug depend on the class it is in and will also vary according to individual circumstances. Class A drugs carry the highest penalty, class C the lowest.

First offenders who are charged with possessing drugs for their own use may only be reprimanded, warned or fined. But even a reprimand means a criminal record. Regular offenders, people selling drugs or drug smugglers can be sentenced to life imprisonment for trafficking. In England and Wales children under 18 are dealt with by a youth court. This court can fine parents or put the offender in detention but not prison.

It is an offence to allow anyone on your premises to produce, give away or sell illegal drugs. It's an offence even to offer to supply the drug free of charge. So if a parent knows that their child is sharing drugs with a friend in their house and does nothing to stop it, the parent has committed an offence. Allowing the smoking of cannabis in your home is also an offence. To stop someone committing an offence with a drug, you can either destroy it or hand it over to the police.

⊕ In groups

Discuss what you think of the arguments to legalise all drugs put forward by the campaigning group Transform (right).

THE PENALTIES

Class A drugs	Maximum penalties
cocaine, crack, ecstasy, heroin, LSD, magic mushrooms, speed (if prepared for injection)	**for possession:** 7 years and a fine **for supply:** life imprisonment and a fine
Class B drugs	**Maximum penalties**
cannabis, speed	**for possession:** 5 years and a fine **for supply:** 14 years and a fine
Class C drugs	**Maximum penalties**
tranquillisers	**for possession:** 2 years and a fine **for supply:** 5 years and a fine

⊕ In groups

Study the information in the sections 'What about the law?' and 'The penalties'.

1. Do you agree that some drugs should carry harsher punishments than others? Why/why not?

2. Do you think imprisonment is a satisfactory deterrent for either drug users or drug suppliers? Give reasons for your views.

3. How can parents teach their children to behave responsibly with regard to drugs?

Why legalising all drugs is the answer

For too long policy makers have used the prohibition of drugs as a smokescreen to avoid addressing the social and economic factors that lead people to use drugs. Most illegal and legal drug use is recreational. Poverty and despair are at the root of most problematic drug use and it is only by addressing these underlying causes that we can hope to significantly decrease the number of problematic users.

Legalising drugs would also eliminate the criminal market place. The market for drugs is demand-led and millions of people demand illegal drugs. Making the production, supply and use of some drugs illegal creates a vacuum into which organised crime moves. The profits are worth billions of pounds. Legalisation would force organised crime from the drugs trade, starve them of income and enable us to regulate and control the market, for example by prescription, licensing, laws on sales to children and advertising regulations.

Most of the violence associated with illegal drug dealing is caused by its illegality. Legalisation would enable us to regulate the market, determine a much lower price and remove users' need to raise funds through crime. Our legal system would be freed up and our prison population dramatically reduced, saving billions.

Time for a *change* in the law?

Cannabis is the most commonly used illegal drug in the UK. Some people would like to see the law changed so it was no longer an offence to use cannabis. For others, legalising cannabis would be a backward step that would lead to more drug problems.

Legalisation would put cannabis in a similar category to alcohol and cigarettes. There still could be laws regulating sales and use but it would not be illegal to use or supply cannabis.

Decriminalisation is slightly different and means it would not be an offence to have small quantities of cannabis for personal use but production and supply would still be illegal.

From Life Files: Drugs

Cannabis factfile

The effects

> 'It makes me feel laid back.' Jake (12)
>
> 'It gives you a nice feeling with no side effects.' Paul (13)
>
> 'It makes me feel calm, especially when my mum's going on at me.' Linda (14)
>
> 'I only tried it once and it was disgusting. I felt dizzy and then I got really sick.' Julie (14)

> Cannabis tends to make people feel more relaxed and confident.
> Some people claim it makes them more creative and thoughtful.
> Others claim it helps them calm down.
> It has no effect on some people.
> It lowers the blood pressure.
> It is non-addictive.
> Effects depend on the user's frame of mind at the time and what their expectations are.

The dangers

> Regular users are likely to be sleepy, clumsy and unable to perform to their best abilities, so the likelihood of accidents increases.
> Because cannabis in food takes longer to get into the bloodstream, you can never be sure how much you are taking in or how strong the cannabis is.
> If the drug is too strong, you can be extremely sick.
> Drinking alcohol with the drug can make you pass out.
> Some users experience paranoia.
> Some users feel anxious and restless when they smoke.
> There is some evidence that long-term cannabis use causes lasting damage to your concentration and memory.
> Smoking cannabis long-term causes a higher risk of respiratory disease, including lung cancer, than smoking.

Adapted from Wise Guides: Drugs, by Anita Naik

Bishop: Teach young people how to use cannabis

Young people should be taught to use cannabis in moderation, the Bishop of Edinburgh said yesterday, fuelling the debate over whether soft drugs should be decriminalised.

The Most Reverend Richard Holloway, head of the Scottish Episcopal Church, equated the drugs debate to that which led to votes for women and said that banning cannabis was akin to banning cream sherry.

'I don't think it can be seen as a crime,' the Bishop told Radio Scotland. 'Something that people want to do in enough numbers and which does not harm others is not a crime. Some people for some reason like to drink cream sherry. We may not like it but we would not forbid it.

As long as it is handled in a responsible way and we teach young people to live moderately and to use recreational substances moderately, then that is the wise policy.'

The Bishop's remarks were heavily criticised by John Orr, Chief Constable of Strathclyde, where there have been nearly 100 drug-related deaths so far this year. Mr Orr said: 'Cannabis is the first step down the rocky road to disaster. There is clear evidence that some of these people started on cannabis. They find that they just don't get the buzz out of it and move on to harder drugs.'

Asked specifically about the Bishop's statements, Mr Orr replied: 'He should try telling that to some of the relatives who are left or someone who has been assaulted or slashed when blurred behaviour has led to attacks.'

From The Independent

In groups

1. Read the newspaper report (left). Decide what you would say in response to the Bishop and Mr Orr.
2. What are the arguments for and against changing the law on cannabis?

In pairs

'I don't want to smoke dope, but I hate being the odd one out. My friends don't force me but they go off to a room to smoke and I get left out. Even when they're not smoking it's horrible, because they're always talking about how brilliant it is.' *Gina (12)*

'There's a boy who sells grass at our school. He's always coming up to us and saying we won't regret it if we try some.' *Yvonne (13)*

Work out what advice you would give to Gina and Yvonne.

A **firm** stand?

Dennis Packer is a parent and a governor. He has become involved because he is determined that there is not going to be a drug problem at his son's school. The head teacher admits that there have been incidents of cannabis smoking and children bringing unidentified tablets into school. The head has dealt with them far too mildly by Mr Packer's standards. Mr Packer wants the school to toughen up on drugs. He is planning to go to the local newspaper before the next governor's meeting and tip them off about the drug problems there have been at the school. He tells himself he's being public spirited and hopes that the publicity will force the

Dennis Packer
(parent and School Governor)

head teacher into taking a firm stand. Mr Packer is sure that in this way he'll be able to get exclusion on the agenda and into the school's drug policy: from now on, it will be 'Fool with drugs and you're out.'

Joyce Williams is the head teacher. She knows that there's been a bit of a drugs problem, but doesn't think it is anything very serious. She believes an open dialogue with the youngsters is the best way of dealing with things. She's planning a term-long drug study in the summer, and is just finding out what outside trainers and drama groups they could involve, so that she can put a proposal before the next governors' meeting. She expects resistance only from Dennis Packer, who is always trying to force a hard line of punishment on drug incidents. Joyce wonders what he would think if he knew that his son, Steve, was one of the lads caught with cannabis recently. The boy begged her not to tell his dad, and they discussed the matter at length. They made a bargain: she told him to research and present a lesson on cannabis to his class. He had really entered into the spirit of the thing and his presentation was so good that she had asked him to repeat it for assembly. She hopes she did the right thing in not telling his father.

Steve Packer
(Dennis Packer's son)

Joyce Williams
(head teacher)

From *Drugs Scene: Community Education and Arts Project*

From an article in T2,
The Daily Telegraph

In groups

Read 'A firm stand?' and discuss the following questions.

1. What issues do you think are important in this situation?
2. Whose point of view do you think is the most sensible? Is someone 'wrong' and someone 'right'?
3. What do you think is likely to happen? What do you think any of the individuals or all the characters in the situation should do?
4. Discuss your school's policy on drugs in school and say why you agree or disagree with it.

Schools and drugs – what do you think?

> " I accept that pupils should be expelled for drug-dealing in schools, but it makes me furious that schools are throwing out kids they find smoking a joint in the changing rooms. The only thing that schools can do is attempt to help those caught.
>
> One way, perhaps, would be to encourage them to talk to older pupils who are ex-drug users themselves. Teenagers need someone they can identify with, someone who can tell them first-hand what a waste of time it is. "
>
> *Jennifer Amory, aged 20*

for your folder Write about how you think schools should deal with drug incidents.

The addict's story – paying for his habit

Dave is 21. He has just finished a three-year prison sentence for burglary and possessing drugs, and is now struggling to build a new life for himself …

Cannabis, ecstasy, speed, cocaine, heroin. I've done the lot, and I'll tell you here and now, I wish I hadn't.

I smoked my first cigarette when I was just 13. Nearly coughed my guts up. But I got used to it, and before long I couldn't do anything unless I had a fag in my mouth. Fags are expensive when you're that age, though. So I had to pinch them, mostly off my mum. Then I started drinking. Cider first, then beer, then spirits. I got used to that, too, and I started nicking bottles of vodka out of shops. This bloke caught me once and chased me down the street.

When I was 14, I got hold of some cannabis. Soon after that some mates got hold of a bit of speed. We had a whale of a time and I was getting a bit of a reputation. I was always a cocky kid and I'd try anything, do anything. It was only because I was shy and insecure really, and I wanted everybody to think I was some sort of hardcase, that I was cool, confident and clever, when actually I was none of those things. I just wanted a bit of attention.

I left school when I was 16 without a qualification to my name. I used to like art, but in the end I couldn't even be bothered with that. And by that time I had a regular habit for ecstasy and cocaine, as well as the fags and booze.

No one would give me a job. To be honest, I was useless. But a friend of a friend offered me a room in his flat, so I moved there. Before I knew what was going on, I was doing heroin. It made me sick as first, but then the buzz was great and I was sick when I wasn't doing it.

The thing about heroin is you need more and more. So me and this bloke start selling dope to school kids to make the money for more heroin. We could never make enough though, so we put our heads together and decided we ought to try a bit of burglary.

So we started breaking into houses near by. We'd watch them for when people were out. Then we'd go in and take out anything we could carry and that we could sell. Anything we couldn't sell, we kept for the flat. Trouble is, you nick a £250 TV, you only get £50 for it if you're lucky. It paid for the drugs for a while, but we always wanted more and we never had enough money. So we'd have to go and nick more.

This went on for a while when early one morning the police came and broke the door down. Turns out the friend of a friend had a previous conviction. They matched his prints to sets they'd found at a break-in a couple of streets away. So they come in, they find all this gear, they find our stash of cannabis and they find me.

I got three years and now I'm out of prison and I've got to find some way of starting all over again. It's not going to be easy, but I won't make the mistake of doing drugs again.

From *Check It!*, Metropolitan Police

In pairs

Talk about what Dave says about why he started taking drugs, and how they affected his life. What further problems did Dave's drugtaking habit lead him into? What does he say was the worst part of his experiences?

Heroin factfile

The effects

> In small doses, heroin gives the user a sense of warmth and well being.

> Higher doses can make them drowsy and relaxed.

> Excessive amounts can result in overdose, coma and in some cases death.

> First time use often leads to side-effects like dizziness and vomiting.

The dangers

> Heroin is very addictive. Getting the next fix can dominate a user's life.

> Tolerance develops, which means the user needs more heroin to get the same effect.

> Users who form a habit may end up taking the drug just to feel normal.

> Those who start by smoking or snorting heroin sometimes switch to injections to maximise the high.

> Injecting can damage veins and lead to gangrene.

> Sharing needles or syringes puts users at risk of dangerous infections like hepatitis and HIV.

> When not on the drug, users have severe withdrawal symptoms, including anxiety, cramps, fever, sweating and severe muscle spasms. This is called going 'cold turkey' and is often so hard to get through that users go back to taking heroin, even when they can no longer get any good effects from it, just so they can avoid having these withdrawal symptoms.

> Heroin users are more likely to resort to crime, stealing to support their expensive heroin habit, which can cost tens of thousands of pounds a year.

Adapted from *The Score: Facts about Drugs*. Health Education Authority

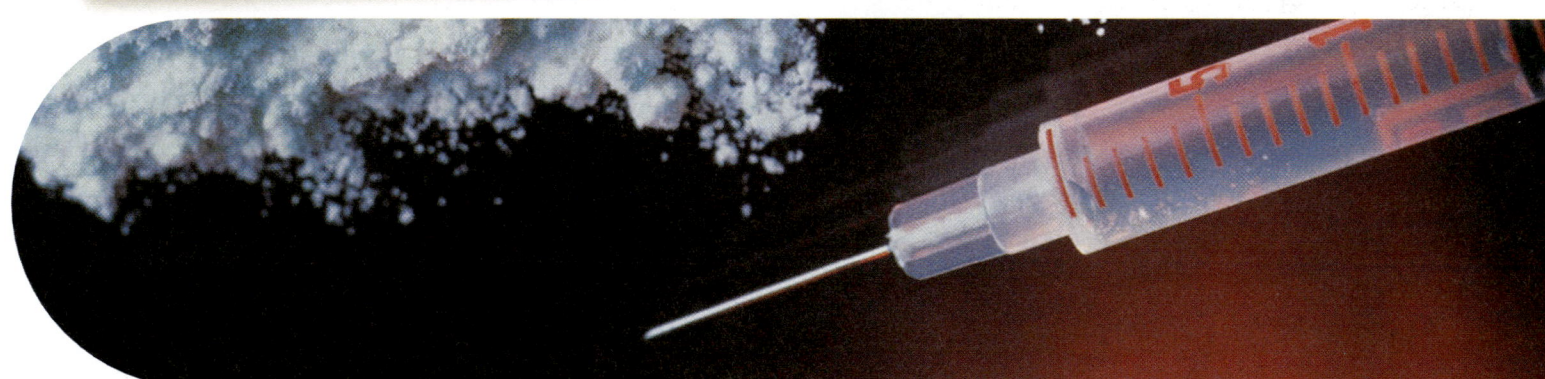

Heroin users getting younger

The average age at which teenagers begin experimenting with heroin has fallen to only 15, two years younger than in the late 1980s, according to new research for a leading drugs charity.

Alarmingly, heroin no longer has the kind of stigma for young teenagers that prevented previous generations experimenting on a large scale. Most try heroin at a friend's house and begin by smoking it. Most abusers move rapidly to weekly then to daily use.

'These heroin users were initially very naive and ill-informed about heroin. They did not understand its subtle potency and addictiveness and had little idea where a heroin career might take them. As habits grow, injecting becomes routine, health and self-esteem suffer and multiple drug use looms, involving cannabis, tranquillisers, methadone and crack cocaine,' the report says.

From an article in *The Guardian*

> The thing I like now is waking up in the morning and having a choice. When you're on heroin, you wake up and the first thing you think of is where you're going to get money to score.
>
> Heroin promises you the world but it takes away every bit of dignity and self-respect you ever had. It just smashes up every hope and dream you have for the future.

Jolene, 17, ex-heroin addict

 ### In groups

1. Discuss your responses to the article 'Heroin users getting younger'.

2. Why do you think some people are ignorant about heroin and its effects? Talk about what people need to know about heroin and how this information could be communicated.

Friends and Relationships

Forming close relationships

During your teenage years, you are likely to meet someone to whom you are particularly attracted. Many teenagers experience for the first time a close relationship with a member of the opposite sex. Close relationships don't just happen. You need to work at them and they need to be based on friendship and commitment.

Being in love

What do we mean when we talk about 'being in love'?

Love is a complicated emotion. Nobody has ever really understood what love is – yet it plays a huge part in most people's lives.

We use the word love in all kinds of ways. We might say that we love someone's clothes, or a TV programme. This is obviously not the same as saying that we love a member of our family, or a special friend.

Feeling love for somebody means that we care about their well-being. Strength of feeling can't be easily measured. You will feel more strongly for some people than others. Sometimes people say that they love somebody, when what they actually feel is infatuation. This is similar to a crush, but can be very intense. It can make you forget about everything and everyone else. Similarly, we can confuse loving somebody with feeling dependent on them.

Sometimes it is easy to confuse love with romance. Love is more than candlelit dinners and bunches of flowers. It is a commitment to another person. It means being prepared to share bad times as well as enjoying good ones, and being able to offer support to one another when problems arise.

From Relationships by Pete Sanders and Steve Myers

 In groups

1. Discuss what 'being in love' means.
2. What is the difference between love and infatuation?
3. Why do people fall in love?

What do you look for in a romantic relationship?

 In groups

On your own write down the main things you would look for in a romantic relationship, then compare your ideas in a group discussion. Are girls' expectations any different from boys' expectations?

Discuss the findings of the American survey into the qualities that boys look for in girls and the qualities that girls look for in boys (right). Suggest any other qualities that you would like a boy/girlfriend of yours to have.

What boys look for

A lot of girls mistakenly feel that most boys who are interested in them are seeking a sexual relationship. But an American survey has shown this to be untrue.

In the survey, when boys were asked 'What are the most important qualities that a girl must have for you to want to go out with her?' the following were the ten most frequently mentioned qualities:

1. Good looks and a good body, but not necessarily stunning – 'and if she has an awful personality I won't ask her again'.
2. Friendly and not conceited, 'a girl who is willing to show that she likes me'.
3. Intelligence.
4. Sense of humour.
5. Honest, 'doesn't play games or tease'.
6. A good conversationalist, 'she has to be able to talk to me'.
7. Similar interests and values.
8. Sexually candid and frank, 'I wouldn't like her to be a prude, but on the other hand I don't want her to have been out with a lot of other boys'.
9. Outgoing, not shy.
10. Mature, 'I'd like her to have a serious side too'.

What girls look for

According to the survey, the most important qualities that a boy must have for a girl to go out with him are:

1. Intelligence.
2. Good looks and good body but not necessarily handsome.
3. A good conversationalist, 'easy to talk to'.
4. Sincere and honest, 'not just out for sex'.
5. Confident, but not conceited.
6. Sense of humour and fun to be with.
7. Clean cut, 'well groomed, doesn't take drugs or drink alcohol to excess'.
8. Romantic and affectionate.
9. Popular at school.
10. Gentle, 'doesn't feel that he has to prove that he's a man'.

From Every Girl's Lifeguide by Dr Miriam Stoppard

Sharing your thoughts and feelings

For a relationship to develop, you must be prepared to share your thoughts and feelings. That means you must be yourself. If you put on an act in order to impress somebody, don't be surprised if they stop being impressed when they find out about the real you.

If you never talk about yourself, you'll find it hard to make close friends. But if you talk about yourself too much, then you are likely to put people off. The skill lies in deciding when to share your thoughts and feelings with somebody in order to get closer to them, so that they will want to share their thoughts and feelings with you.

> ### Be yourself
> When you first start going out with someone, you will want to make a good impression. Wanting someone to like you and not being sure how they feel can make you very nervous and awkward. You may not know how to behave or what to say. You may even behave in a way you normally wouldn't, in order to gain approval. It is more helpful to try to relax and just be yourself.

Pete Sanders and Steve Myers, *Relationships*

Talking openly

> I think most boys and girls are conscious from an early age of a feeling of separateness between the sexes. Perhaps this feeling has become less strong now, but I still feel that we're programmed in our relationships with boys – we can't talk to them as if they were simply other human beings. You tend to do and say what you think you are supposed to be doing and saying.

Lisa

In groups

Discuss the points Lisa makes.

1. Are you conscious of a feeling of separateness between the sexes?
2. Do you feel that you are programmed in your relationships with members of the opposite sex?
3. Do you agree that 'you tend to do and say what you think you are supposed to be doing and saying' in your relationships with members of the opposite sex?
4. Is it easier to talk openly about yourself, your problems and your hopes or fears, to someone of your own sex? If so, why?

Seeing it their way

For any relationship to be successful, there's got to be a certain amount of give and take. Unless you are prepared to see the other person's point of view, you are bound to have arguments.

Look at it from my point of view

There's a film that Susan and Roy both want to see. It's on for two more days – Saturday and Sunday.

They've arranged to go to the cinema on Saturday evening. On Saturday afternoon, Roy phones Susan to fix up a time to meet. Susan says she's awfully sorry, but her uncle and aunt have just announced that they are coming that evening. Susan's mother wants her to stay in and see them. Besides, Susan hasn't seen them for ages, and they get on well together. Couldn't she and Roy go to the cinema on Sunday instead?

However, Roy has arranged to go on a fishing trip on Sunday with his mate Trev. He doesn't want to let Trev down. The last time Roy had to cry off at the last minute because he was doing something with Susan and he doesn't want to let Trev down again. He's not prepared to risk losing Trev's friendship, as Trev knows someone in the local angling club who can get discounts on fishing gear.

Role play

Role play the phone conversation between Susan and Roy. Do it twice. First, do it so that Susan and Roy each give their own viewpoints so strongly that they don't listen to what the other one is saying. They end up having a blazing row.

Then, repeat the conversation. This time, Susan and Roy make every effort to see the other person's point of view. They try to work out a compromise that they are both willing to accept.

In pairs

Discuss Sonia's problem (below) and draft Melissa's reply to him.

> *Dear Melissa*
>
> *I really like my boyfriend, but he bosses me about. We always do what he wants to do and he expects me always to agree with him. I'm worried that if I say anything to him, he'll end our relationship and I'd be heartbroken if that happened. I don't know what to do.*
>
> *Sonia*

What makes a relationship work?

No two relationships are alike. Nobody can guarantee how each will turn out. There are, however, several factors which most people agree contribute to a successful relationship.

Being able to talk about feelings and ideas, and really listening to the other person are essential. People in long-term relationships often talk about the importance of working together through any problems which come up. This is better than ignoring difficulties, and hoping they will go away. It is necessary to be able to forgive others, and not bear grudges. In any relationship we have to know when to step back and allow others time and space to sort out their feelings. If someone feels restricted by another person, they may grow to resent the relationship.

Trust and honesty are vital if a close relationship is going to succeed. Being open about your feelings allows the other person to get to know you well, and lets you share your experiences. Keeping secrets or not being able to talk to each other can cause problems. Many people who enjoy successful relationships say it is important to allow people to be themselves. They do not believe in trying to change the other person.

Relationships are not fixed. They change over time. We are always meeting new people, or finding out new things about those we already know. People in relationships should not be seen as possessions. We all need space to express ourselves. It would be boring if everything and everybody stayed the same. People are always developing new interests and going in different directions. This is what makes relationships exciting.

From Relationships by Pete Sanders and Steve Myers

 In groups

1. Read the article 'What makes a relationship work?' Discuss the factors which the authors say help to make relationships work.
2. Talk about how relationships may change and develop over time, and why it is important to allow your boyfriend/girlfriend their own space.

What to do if your boyfriend is jealous

Even if you are head over heels in love with the boy, did you really expect to have to spend every minute of your day with him? Did you plan to ditch all your other friends so as to keep him happy? Not likely. The suffocating relationship that results from having a jealous boyfriend is not a good relationship.

To get your boyfriend to release his stranglehold on your social life, you have to do the following:

1. Talk to him about the problem. Make it clear to him that as a boyfriend he's wonderful but as a friend he's the pits. Tell him that a good friend would never think of controlling a friend's life.

2. Reassure him that he is just as important as your friends. If you say that he's more important, you are playing right into his possessive hands.

3. Don't encourage any sort of jealous behaviour by playing your boyfriend off against your friends. The poor guy is obviously insecure and it wouldn't take much to freak him out.

4. Let him know that what happens in your relationship is simply between you and him. If he suspects that you are blabbing the details of every snog to your friends, then is it any wonder that he's trying to keep you away from them?

5. If all this tact and diplomacy doesn't change your boyfriend's jealous behaviour then the relationship is doomed.

From Friends or Enemies? by Anita Naik

Breaking up

Sometimes, as time passes, two people realize that they have simply grown out of love with each other – being together is no longer what's best for them both.

However and whenever the moment of breaking up comes, the best bet is to handle it carefully and with respect for both yourself and him. Just because you no longer love each other doesn't mean that you shouldn't care for each other any more – after all, you've had some really good times together so don't try to make out that all that time was wasted.

Break up, not make up

So how do you know when it is time to break up rather than make up?

If you have had a big argument about something, think hard about what it was all about – and think fairly too!

- ⊙ Was it something that he said or did?
- ⊙ Did he get bent out of shape because of something you said to his friends?
- ⊙ Should one of you apologise?

If the answer is an apology, and if you believe that you are really in love with him, then think hard about being the one to apologise. If it's up to your boyfriend to say sorry, don't make it difficult for him when he does try. If you don't let him apologise and you split up as a result, you'll only have yourself to blame later on when you start to regret that you are no longer an item.

On the other hand, maybe you don't really want to make up with your boyfriend.

- ⊙ Have you had just too many arguments?
- ⊙ Do you think that he's no longer much fun to be with?
- ⊙ Does he spend too much time with his friends and not enough with you?

If any of these things are true, don't let your relationship drag on indefinitely if it's not what you want. Be strong enough to bring the relationship to an end rather than dragging it on when it's going nowhere.

Rules of breaking up

Let's face it, breaking up is hard to do for both parties, but there are some ways of handling the situation that can make it better. Here are some golden rules of breaking up:

- ⊙ <u>Tell the truth</u>. Don't think you can make the situation better by saying something like, 'I think we need a break and then we can get back together again in a few months.'
- ⊙ <u>Be kind</u>. Don't be tempted to say, 'Well, I never really liked you anyway.' Just try to make it easier for yourself. Don't say things that you don't mean or which you know aren't true.

- ⊙ <u>Don't go out with someone else before you split up</u>. Even if you like someone else, you should end one relationship before starting with another boy. That way you should minimize the hurt for all of you – and help keep your reputation intact!
- ⊙ <u>Don't tell tales</u>. When you split up, don't start telling other people your boyfriend's secrets and the things he told you in private. It is just plain mean. And worse

still, he could get his own back and start doing the same to you.

- ⊙ <u>Stay cool</u>. Although you may be tempted, do NOT create a big scene by insulting each other. Do your best to avoid any kind of ranting and raving. And try to control your voice – and that temper too! You'll come out for the better in the end.
- ⊙ <u>Don't break up in front of your friends</u>. Don't even think about a public showdown – under any circumstances.
- ⊙ <u>Keep clear of him</u>. Once you've actually broken up, don't hang around in the same places where you used to go with him – at least for a while anyway. Give each other some space to get used to the split.
- ⊙ <u>Don't break up if you don't mean it</u>. You'll hurt him really badly if you expect him to take you back at a later date. And he may hurt you by telling you something you don't want to hear.
- ⊙ <u>Don't hide</u>. When you see him in future, even if it's with another girl, don't just ignore him. You'd be better off saying a friendly 'Hi', and then carrying on with whatever you're doing. This shows you're over him and onto your own thing!
- ⊙ <u>Have a good cry</u>. Even if it was you who made the decision to split, you may be feeling really bad. So go ahead and have a good cry on your best friend's shoulder – or maybe alone in your bedroom. You'll probably feel much better after letting go of your emotions.
- ⊙ <u>Write it down</u>. You may also feel better if you write down how you feel. If you feel angry, writing about it could cool you off. If you feel really sad, pouring out your thoughts could clear your head. Whatever your feelings now, writing about them confirms how much the love you used to have meant to you while it was still good.

 In groups

1. Discuss the advice in the article above on how to end a relationship. What do you think are the most important points to remember when breaking off a relationship?

2. What is the best way to announce that you are ending a relationship – over the phone, by letter, through a friend or face to face?

From Love Lines *by Caroline Plaisted*

Same-sex relationships

It is estimated that up to one in ten people are gay. Yet, if you flick though any teenage magazine, most of the articles focus on heterosexual relationships. In addition, until very recently, television and advertising have tended to portray society as if gay men and lesbians do not exist.

Life can be very difficult for gay young men and lesbian young women growing up in a culture which is geared towards heterosexuality. But what is it like for families when young people come out as gay or lesbian? How do parents and siblings cope with the idea – and in the end does it make any differences to relationships within the family?

'I've got something to tell you'

Sarah, 18, describes the reactions of her family when her brother Nathan, 21, announced that he was gay.

I'll never forget the day that my elder brother told us he was gay. It took everyone in the family by surprise.

Like lots of boys, Nathan got bullied when he first started secondary school. But he seemed to cope with it well. He stood up to the worst of the bullies and won a lot of respect for doing so. It made him popular – especially with some of the girls. I can remember one or two of my friends at the time saying how much they fancied him.

So at first, the rest of us in the family couldn't believe it when one Sunday afternoon, when he was 16, he told us he'd something very important to say. We'd just finished lunch and were about to start clearing away, when Nathan suddenly said: 'Wait. There's something you all need to know about me, because it's very important. I'm gay.'

There was a stunned silence. Dad put down the pile of plates he was holding and said: 'Now I've heard it all!' Mum said, 'Don't be ridiculous, Nathan. You're not gay.' My younger brother, Phil, and I just sat there. None of us believed him.

Nathan tried to explain that he'd always known he was gay. But Mum and Dad wouldn't listen to him. Mum kept saying: 'It's just a phase you're going through.' We were all in shock, I suppose.

Things were a bit tense for some days as we all adjusted to the news. In fact, it took Mum and Dad several months to accept that what Nathan had said was true. But eventually they realised that Nathan is serious about his sexuality and now they've got used to it. Mum and Nathan are very close now and she's met his boyfriend, Greg, and she really likes him.

I think it was easier for Phil and me. We talked about it with Nathan and could see that he would just go on being the elder brother we'd always known. Both of us knew that there was no reason for us to feel any differently about Nathan than we'd always felt.

Not long after he'd told us, Nathan told his friends. All of them said they respected him for telling them – except one, and Nathan just shrugged it off, saying that if that was how he felt, then he didn't want him as a friend anyway.

In pairs

Discuss how Sarah and her mum reacted to Nathan telling them that he is gay. What do you learn from Nathan's story about what it is like to be gay and about what may happen when a young person 'comes out'?

Attitudes to homosexuality

There is tremendous pressure on us all to conform; to become objects of desire to the opposite sex, to get married and have children … The problem is intensified by the fact that in our culture there is still a taboo against homosexuality. This taboo exists mainly because there is an old idea that 'sex equals reproduction' and, as loving someone of the same sex can't produce babies, many see it as 'unnatural', 'abnormal', even 'perverted'.

Insulting words such as 'poofter', 'faggot', 'queer', 'bender' and 'dyke' have been invented to reinforce this prejudice and they cause a lot of harm. These prejudices make many gay people feel that if they are attracted to the same sex there must be something wrong with them and they end up feeling bad about themselves and their sexuality.

From The Just Seventeen Advice Book by Rosalyn Chissick

"The Conference … while rejecting homosexual practice as incompatible with Scripture, calls on all our people to minister pastorally and sensitively to all, irrespective of sexual orientation, and to condemn irrational fear of homosexuals."

Lambeth Conference, 1998, Resolution on Human Sexuality (Church of England)

"In Sacred Scripture they [homosexuals] are condemned … This does not permit us to conclude that all those who suffer from homosexuality are personally responsible for it, but it does point to the fact that homosexual acts are disordered and can in no case be approved of."

Persona Humana [Declaration of Sexual Ethics, 29 December 1975] (Roman Catholic)

"For homosexual men and women, permanent relationships characterised by love can be an appropriate and Christian way of expressing their sexuality."

Methodist report

In groups

Discuss your responses to the views expressed in the section 'Attitudes to homosexuality'. Which view or views do you most agree with and why?

Homosexuality – Some questions and answers

I feel certain I'm gay. Should I tell everyone?

Whether or not you tell people that you're gay is entirely up to you. You don't have to make a statement about your sexuality if you don't want to do so. Making a decision whether to 'come out' to your friends and family can be difficult, because you can't be sure what their reaction will be. If you've got perceptive parents and friends you may find out that they have already guessed and are ready to accept you for what you are.

Unfortunately, however, some people aren't so understanding. They may be prejudiced against homosexuality and may find it hard to accept what you're saying.

What are gay people like?

Gay people are just the same as everybody else. The only way that they are different from the majority of other people is that they have a different sexuality.

One reason that people sometimes think that gay people are different is because of the myths about what they are like. One common myth is that all gay men are effeminate. They dress in rather unusual clothes and talk and behave in an affected way. Another common myth is that all lesbians are 'butch'. They dress in men's clothes, such as dungarees and boots, have short haircuts and deep voices. These two stereotypes are, of course, complete nonsense. The vast majority of gay people aren't at all like this. Most gay men and women look the same, dress the same and behave the same as straight men and women.

I've had crushes on people of the same sex. Am I gay?

Having crushes on people of the same sex doesn't necessarily mean you're gay. Lots of teenage boys and girls have crushes on people of the same sex, as well as on people of the opposite sex. Then, as older teenagers and adults, they are straight. The fact is that people change and the feelings you have now may be different from the feelings you'll have in the future. If you have deep feelings and maybe even a sexual relationship with someone of the same sex when you're a teenager, adults are inclined to dismiss it as a phase you are going through. However, there are problems with this attitude, because a lot of gay people discover their sexuality while they are still quite young. It's wrong to dismiss their feelings as just a phase.

I only find people of the same sex attractive, so I think I'm gay. Is there anyone I can talk to about how I feel?

If you think you're gay and need to talk it through with somebody, it's often a good idea to talk to someone who's had a similar experience. You may know someone who's openly gay who you could talk to in confidence. Alternatively, you may prefer to talk to someone who doesn't know you. If that's the case, you can phone a gay helpline. You'll talk to a gay person who's a trained counsellor, who'll be able to offer you advice. You can contact the Lesbian and Gay Switchboard (24 hour service) on 020 7837 7324. They will put you in contact with organisations that specialise in helping young gay and lesbian people.

How can you tell if someone is gay?

From *You and Your Sexuality* by Erica Stewart

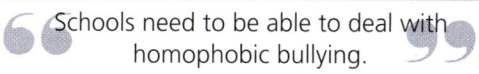 **In groups**

'If gay young people have problems in getting people to accept their sexuality, then the problem is not theirs but the attitudes and prejudices of others.'

Discuss this view.

Homophobic bullying

> We believe that fear or hatred of homosexuals is a social evil, similar to anti-semitism, racism, slavery, and with the same evil consequences. It harms both the victimized individuals, and the society which tolerates it.

Towards a Charter of Homosexual Rights

> Schools need to be able to deal with homophobic bullying.

Dept of Education, Sex and Relationships Education Guidance, July 2000

> 72% of young lesbians and gay men indicated that they had either played truant or feigned illness to avoid homophobic abuse at school.

Stonewall website

Homophobic bullying is the bullying of lesbians and gay men because they are gay. Such bullying is often carried out by people who are unsure of their own sexuality, or threatened by difference. Whatever the case, like all bullying it is unacceptable. It is important to respect others' sexual orientation even if we don't share it or feel uneasy with it.

Homophobic bullying at school

Lately, there have been several major studies into homophobic bullying and its effects. In general, all the studies found a widespread prevalence of homophobic bullying in the classroom and that instances of homophobic bullying often involved more violent attacks than general bullying.

Neil Duncan's research shows that bullying, especially of boys, is widespread in schools. The report is based on observation and interviews with boys and girls between the ages of 11 and 16 at five large comprehensive co-education schools. 16-year-old boys who were interviewed said:

- 'If there were gay kids in this school, I'd move school.'
- 'If my best mate told me he was queer, I'd slap him, I would. I wouldn't have him coming near me.'

The report suggests that teachers do not have the skills to deal with sexual bullying, particularly in relation to sexual orientation: 'If they [teachers] talk about homosexuality they are in fear that a counsellor or parent will complain. It is difficult enough for children to tell a teacher that they have been bullied. It is much more difficult to talk about sexual bullying.'

Adapted from the Stonewall website

Rights and responsibilities

Your Growing Independence

Your parents will have been accepting your developing independence since you were a baby and most parents welcome the approach of maturity, encourage it and are proud of it. However, you may find that your parents are not so positive when you start to strike out for freedom, which can cause friction between you. If this is the case, you will need to use a little bit of tact and subtlety towards them. Unless you plan ahead and introduce your parents gradually to the idea that you want to make decisions for yourself and manage your own life, you may end up having rows and destructive confrontations.

You should try to avoid these at all costs. Introduce your desire for independence in a way that they can understand, for example, ask about what they wanted to do when they were the same age as you, and what their parents allowed them to do. Ask them if they were happy about that situation and how they could have gone about getting more freedom. It should then be easier for your parents to see things from your point of view.

Taking on responsibilities

Your parents will be more eager to accept your independence if you show them that you are responsible and trustworthy. You might, for instance, offer to take on some of the important jobs around the house. If your parents find that they can depend on you to cook the evening meal, to be a good babysitter or to carry out errands efficiently, then they will not only feel like giving you a little more independence but will also want to reward you by trusting your judgement.

One of the best ways to show your parents that you are a responsible person and can see a project through to the end is to take on some kind of part-time job. You could, for instance, take on a paper round when you are still in your early teens, and then later you could find a Saturday job, say, in a shop. This will clearly demonstrate that you are willing to work and that you can be responsible and possibly make a useful contribution to the household finances. Your parents may be grateful for the extra money and they will certainly appreciate your gesture.

Helping around the house

I believe that all children should be doing chores around the house from a very early age. A family should be a team and team members need to help one another and give each other as much support as they can. As children get older, they can take responsibility for more and more difficult jobs and I think you should be on the lookout for opportunities that allow you to do this. Don't always wait for your parents to suggest ways in which you might help, or even for them to be forced to nag you before you take action. If you are observant there are 101 tasks you could take off their plates and their minds. Your parents would be very appreciative if you did a couple of chores on a regular basis, rather than only helping when you're in the mood.

From *Every Girl's Lifeguide* by Dr Miriam Stoppard

Family arguments

The key to making sure arguments with your parents don't ruin your life is communication. This isn't easy when both 'teams', so to speak, have squared up on opposite sides of the field and everyone is on the offensive. Communicating doesn't mean screaming, shouting, making nasty comments or sticking bitchy messages to the fridge. It means listening, as well as talking.

By listening you may see the problem from the other person's perspective. Opening lines of communication also entails being honest. It's no good ranting at your mum about having to wash the dishes, when what you're really mad about is that your sister gets away with more (and does a lot less washing up) than you.

From *Families – Can't Live With Them, Can't Live Without Them!* by Anita Naik

In groups

'My dad is so strict he won't let us go out in the evenings. We have to stay in and study. He even decides what we can watch on TV.' Darren, 15

'My sister and I have to share a room. I'm not allowed to make phone calls and they always know where I am because my dad insists on driving me everywhere and picking me up. I've got no freedom and no privacy.' Emma, 15

'I've got a boyfriend and he keeps wanting to meet my parents. But they're so old-fashioned they think I shouldn't have boyfriends at my age and I'm frightened they'll stop me seeing him.' Teresa, 15

Discuss what advice you'd give to Darren, Emma and Teresa about how to approach their parents and what they should say to their parents that would get them to understand their point of view. Draft a reply to one of them.

In pairs

1. Discuss the advice given in this article and say why you agree or disagree with it. Talk about what responsibilities you are prepared to take on in your family.

2. If you take on a part-time job, who should decide how you use the money you earn? Should you offer to use some of it to pay for things that your parents have previously been paying for?

Your Needs, Rights and Privileges

Some parents accept the argument that you should be allowed the same kind of freedom as your friends. Others do not. I personally feel that while you are living with your parents, you should do as they wish and stick to their rules. You will get nowhere if you deliberately go against what they have said. If you disagree, the only solution is to negotiate with your parents and come to some agreement whereby they give you increasing amounts of freedom while they learn to trust you.

If you think your parents are being unreasonably strict, for instance, more strict than your friends' parents, then tell them that you think you are getting a rough deal, but also say that for the time being you accept this and ask if they would agree to a trial period with more freedom. If everything works out all right, then you could gradually introduce a few more privileges – always on the basis that you keep your promises.

Staying out late

This is a contentious subject for all teenagers, especially girls, largely because their parents tend to be more protective of them than of boys. You can do nothing to prevent this protective attitude, so be understanding and don't fly off the handle when this subject comes up.

Start discussions about it early and gradually. As you get older, you might ask your parents to allow you to stay out a little later if you tell them where you are, if you give them your phone number and if you promise to get home on time, and do so. Then you can justifiably ask them to let you stay out a bit later every few months. If you cheerfully volunteer information about your whereabouts, your parents will be greatly reassured.

Giving parties at home

If you want to hold a party for your friends in your parents house, there are some definite 'do's and 'don'ts' to think about. Remember always that your parents are doing you a big favour by allowing you to hold a party in their house, so you should treat their property with respect and make sure your friends do likewise.

From Every Girl's Lifeguide by Dr Miriam Stoppard

 In groups

1. How late do you think you should be allowed to stay out?

2. Do you agree with the writer of the article that your parents are being protective when they put limits on your staying out late?

 In pairs

1. You have a birthday coming up and you are hoping to have a party at home. You do not want your parents to be there. However, they are concerned about what might happen if they are not there. Work out the discussion you might have with a parent or carer.

2. You are giving out invitations at break in the classroom. Suddenly one of them is snatched by Amy – someone you do not want anywhere near your party. What do you do?

3. Amy arrives at your party. How do you deal with her?

4. In the middle of the party, your parents say they are just going out for a drink. They haven't been gone long when the doorbell rings. It is Amy's boyfriend and several of his friends – and some are already drunk. They say that Amy invited them. How do you deal with the situation?

Your *Own* Space

If space allows, all young people should have a place of their own in the home, a bolt hole where they can retire to and escape from the rest of the world. If you do have your own room, you should be proud of it; apart from anything else, it's a mark of respect for your own privacy by your parents. It can reflect your own personality with its colour scheme, furniture and the way that you decorate it.

Don't forget that you are not living in a hotel – there isn't a maid who comes round to tidy your room each morning – and if it isn't tidied, your mother will almost certainly feel obliged to do it herself. You may well consider this an intrusion, but there is only one way round it: you owe it to the rest of the household to keep your room in a decent state of cleanliness and tidiness. It is not fair for you to say that as it's your room you can keep it as you like, dirt and all. There is no reason why your parents should tolerate your untidy room. It is fair and right for you to conform to their domestic standards while you are living at home.

From Every Girl's Lifeguide by Dr Miriam Stoppard

 In groups

'It's my room. I should be able to keep it as I like.' Discuss this view and say why you agree or disagree with it.

Dealing with a break-up

Each year the parents of thousands of children and teenagers decide to separate or get divorced. In some cases parents who have split up eventually get back together again, but in the majority of cases the break-up is final.

Many of these parents will form a new relationship and over half of them will re-marry within five years. Children whose parents split up often find themselves becoming part of a new family, with a step-parent, who may also have children of their own.

When your parents split up, it inevitably leads to a change in family circumstances. You may have to move home and the parent you live with may be short of money. In some cases, the break-up comes as a relief, for example if your parents have been rowing a lot and the atmosphere has become almost intolerable. Even in these cases, though, for most young people there is also a certain amount of pain and unhappiness.

Coping with your parents' separation or divorce is difficult whatever the circumstances and people's experiences vary enormously. Even within the same family, one young person may find it much easier to adjust to the change than another. The process of adapting to the new situation can take a considerable length of time.

⊕ In groups

1. What do you learn from Robina's story about the different emotions children experience when their parents split up? Talk about how Robina's feelings have altered and changed as she has become used to her parents living apart.

2. If your parents are planning to split up, is it better to tell everyone or to keep it to yourself?

3. How important do you think it is to keep in contact with both your parents if they separate? Is it always desirable, whatever the circumstances?

Robina's story

Robina Hussain, 14, lives with her mother in North London. Her parents split up three years ago.

I have always felt sorry for kids whose parents are divorced or separated. The parents both go their separate ways while the kids are left to choose between them. I believe that when a man and a woman get married they should stay together through thick and thin. If not for themselves, then for the sake of their children. The parents can go away and find new partners, but the children can't …

The date of my parents' divorce was 15 November 1997. My dad had been getting more and more moody, and in the end it was Mum who asked for the divorce … I was eleven when it happened and I cried all night until my twelfth birthday … I remember thinking that my birthday would make me feel better. But it didn't. Dad told us that he was remarrying and that we would have a stepmother, two stepsisters (twins), and a stepbrother. He thought I would be happy because I'd have another family … But it was just another one of my beliefs down the drain. I believed that you should only marry once …

Dad begged me to go to his wedding, but I was so angry I refused. My sisters, cousins, aunts and uncles went … When my sisters came back from the wedding they were so excited they couldn't stop talking about my dad's new wife, Sameera. From the way they were talking I knew they would be moving in with my dad and Sameera … To tell you the truth, I'd rather have lived with my dad, but I felt responsible for my mum …

I think at that time I was pretty jealous of my dad and his new family. There were eight of them and only two of us. The thought of my dad being with another woman was totally weird. I was also worried that I wouldn't get as much attention, but at least I had Mum all to myself and we weren't totally forgotten by the others. My sisters visited every week and still do … My stepsisters and stepbrother came to visit too. To begin with, I used to run upstairs to my room to hide when they arrived and didn't come out until they had gone.

I had to come out of hiding when Mum went to Pakistan on her own for seven months. I was anxious because I'd thought Sameera was like a wicked stepmother and I was stressed out, thinking, what if Dad doesn't like me anymore? What if they leave me out? But they didn't, they treated me exactly as if I was one of them …

After that, I actually started to have some fun. We all began to act like a real family. It felt really good to be with my sisters, brothers, Dad and new Mum – yes, I even began to see Sameera as a mother …

When my mum came back, I didn't really want to part from the new family I'd joined and go to my single parent. So I was kind of mixed up. I wanted to cry and for a while I thought it would be like going through the divorce all over again – but it wasn't …

Now, as a fourteen-year-old teenager, I can't really imagine how life would be if both my parents were together … I have got most of my life sorted now, I spend weekends round my dad's and weekdays with my mum … It's fun. I've got my mum all to myself and we've become really good friends … I have learnt a big lesson from this experience. Instead of locking myself away from my troubles, I have learnt that if I face them and come out of hiding I can actually start having fun.

Extract from 'Smile' by Ruby Khan. Taken from *Family Fallout: Young Women Talk about Family Break Up* edited by Helen Hines

1. What do you think are the main reasons why so many couples separate and get divorced?

2. One in three marriages ends in divorce. Do you think it is too easy to get divorced?

3. Should parents always explain to their children the reasons why they are separating?

4. When parents separate who should decide where the children are going to live? How much say should a child have? Does it depend on the age of the child?

A poll carried out for *The Guardian* newspaper in August 2000 found that 64% of people said that unhappy parents should split up. But what's best for the children?

FOR THE CHILD'S SAKE

by Adrienne Katz

'Having two homes is like putting your life in a couple of carrier bags every week,' says Selina, 16, whose parents have split up. But in the swirling debate about whether parents should stick together for the sake of the children, young people like Selina hardly get a look in.

The 'experts', like the parents, are divided into two warring camps. There are those who argue, based on a large body of research, that conflict in the home is harmful. On the other hand, based on equally valid evidence, there are those who say resposible adults should 'think of the children' and keep on working at their relationship.

The truth, as usual, is more complex. With so much attention focused on the breakdown of the traditional family, the issue of how good a job parents are doing is often overlooked. How well are they handling the split? What arrangements have they made for the children? Is their depression affecting their parenting?

One recent study suggested 'the absence of a parent figure is not the most influential feature of separation for children's

development'. The authors pointed out that separation is part of a process beginning long before the split itself and continuing long after. For a minority there are greater risks than for those in intact families, but communication, contact, reassurance and stability will limit long-term difficulties.

Indeed, living for years in an unhappy

family can affect children more than the split itself. Although Bobby is only eight years old, he agrees. 'It was good when they splitted up because they used to argue a lot … It's better now, lots better.' It's better too for the large number of mothers who want to remove their children from domestic violence.

Some of the most recent research has at last begun to focus on the child's experience and feelings, as opposed to simply assessing the 'outcome'. What's interesting is that children actually seldom seem to care what form their family takes and whether or not there are pieces of paper holding it together. Hope, 14, insists, 'My family just is. It's different from other people's families, but I don't mind because who says what a family should be like?'

David, 15, agrees: 'I was a bit upset at first but you learn to live with it. When I look back it's probably the best thing for us, and the way we live now is fine. It makes no difference really.'

Would being consulted and not excluded from the process help some young people to feel less isolated in the chaos? Ursula, 18, says: 'The children should get a say and the parents should be able to sort things out for everyone – they should be able to act

◐ **In pairs**

1. What do you think of the ideas discussed by Adrienne Katz in the article (above)? Do you think children benefit from a split if their parents' relationship is full of conflict or unhappiness? Or do you think that parents should stay together for the sake of the children? Give your reasons.

2. Draw up a list of 'Dos and Don'ts' offering children advice on how to cope when their parents split up.

⇐ **Feedback**

Share your ideas about the effects that parents choosing either to stay together or to separate has on children.

for your folder Write an article for a teenage magazine about the changes that may occur in a young person's life if their parents split up, and how to cope with them.

Coping with grief

Throughout our lives we learn to love people and to depend upon them. So when they die, we go through a whole series of emotions to try and make sense of what has happened.

In some societies, death is not talked about or celebrated. It is endured privately with a deep sense of loss. In such cases the first emotion will be one of shock. Those who are left behind feel helpless. They want to deny that anything has happened. This feeling may turn to anger since they are now alone – left to fend for themselves. Of course, the anger is especially strong when it is a young person who dies since it seems such a waste of life. The anger may even be mixed with guilt as they think back to things they might have done to improve the relationship or make things happen differently. Sometimes a sense of depression takes over when it is difficult to find direction, and only as time passes, and new experiences flood in, does a feeling of growing acceptance take over.

Although grief is an emotion of the mind, all strong feelings have an effect on our bodies. Most people find that crying offers release from tension. The symptoms of grief may come in waves. At worst, there is a sense of panic which will automatically release adrenalin into the body. Grief often brings temporary indigestion and heartburn, sleeplessness, a loss of appetite, a feeling of tension in the head, and as a result of all this, irritable and jumpy behaviour.

It may be difficult to do, but keeping busy and active helps people to get over grief. Time alone doesn't heal. Only the events that fill time can do that. Any activity, particularly real exercise, will reduce physical stress, since this stimulates the production of glucose and energy.

A bereaved person needs time and a great deal of understanding to get over a death. They may need to talk to a sympathetic ear. It's essential to appreciate how vital it is to allow a person to grieve and mourn.

From Growing Up

The death of a parent

How you will feel

It's normal to have lots of different feelings after the death of someone close to you. At first you may feel shock, then denial (you can't accept that it's happened), then anger, and finally sadness and depression. You may feel so miserable that you just want to withdraw from the world, not wanting to speak, see anyone or do anything. You may just want to sit in your own room and think. Many hours can pass quite quickly while you're in this mood, and comfort from brothers and sisters and the rest of the family doesn't seem to mean anything. You may not want to go to school or even to go out; you'll just want to be alone with your thoughts.

For a few weeks this is perfectly normal and you should ask people to let you go through this state of grieving and shock on your own if you want to. However, at the end of two weeks or so you might want to start getting back to your normal routine. Try to mix in with the family again and go out occasionally, perhaps to see a film. It's a good idea also to organize your school books and sports gear so that you can make an attempt to start ordinary living again. However, remember that if you continue to feel low and depressed for some time, it's not abnormal.

What you can do

Crying can help. Sometimes crying together with your Mum or Dad can help both of you. You'll probably come across your parent doing something and crying at the same time. Don't be embarrassed, just go across and hold your Mum or Dad: this can bring you closer together than you were before, you'll comfort each other and  be stronger afterwards. Having a family chat now and then can help you get your feelings out in the open. You can talk about what's happened, how you feel and what you're going to do for the future. There's a lot of truth in the old saying, 'a trouble shared is a trouble halved', so you'll just feel a lot better for having talked about your feelings. You may find that your brothers and sisters are feeling exactly the same as you and you won't feel so alone.

Keeping a diary is a great comfort, too. Your diary can be like a friend who'll listen to you without arguing. You can put a lot of your secret thoughts down on paper when it's too difficult to talk about them. It's a huge relief to get those thoughts out of your mind. Once they're in the diary, it's as though you've dealt with them: they're over and you don't have to experience the pain any more.

From Every Girl's Lifeguide by Dr Miriam Stoppard

⊕ In groups

What do you learn from the two articles on this page about the emotions people are likely to feel when someone dies, and about how to cope with them?

? For research

Use the resources centre to find out about the different funeral procedures and mourning customs in different cultures.

⇄ Feedback

Discuss together what you found out about how different cultures deal with death.

The death of a friend

When Tara's best friend died, she found it very hard to cope…

'My best friend, Alison, died in October last year of bone cancer. At her funeral everybody said what a tragedy it was for Alison and her family but nobody mentioned me – yet me and Ali had been friends since we were five. At school, girls kept bursting into tears saying they were missing her and I wanted to hit them because some of them had hardly even known her. People started talking about her like she was a saint and saying things they remembered about her and how she was such a laugh. Half of me was pleased to hear them say that, but half of me wanted to shout that they didn't know her as well as I did, and no way was she perfect, she was just … Ali.

I started to hate school. I didn't have a best friend any more and had no one to hang around with. Other girls seemed scared to speak to me, and I was frightened to make new mates in case Ali's mum and dad thought I was forgetting her already.

Finally, Mum spoke to me about how I was feeling and she persuaded me to talk to Ali's parents. They were really nice to me and also put me in charge of a collection at school in Ali's memory, which showed I was her special friend.

I still haven't got another best friend, though I do feel I'm coping better. I can think about Ali now without crying. But I still miss her very much.' Tara, 14

Our advice

We all expect to feel sad when someone dies, but it's quite common to feel angry too.

Tara wanted people to realise how upset she was over Ali. That's understandable, but although the other girls who were upset weren't close to Ali, just knowing someone who suddenly dies can be a big shock, especially when it's someone your own age.

When people know you've lost someone you loved sometimes they're too scared to mention that person in case they upset you. But if you feel that talking about the person would help you, say so – sharing memories can be a big step towards coping.

Another helpful idea is to do something positive, like Tara did when she organised a collection in Ali's name. Finding out more about the illness that someone died from or fund-raising for a charity to help others who suffer can make you feel less helpless.

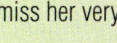

From *Shout* © D.C. Thomson & Co. Ltd

Helping a Bereaved Friend

If you know someone who has just lost a loved one, there are a number of things you can do to make it easier for them and you:

▶ Don't be afraid to talk to them. You don't have to say anything apart from 'I'm sorry' and put your arm around them.

▶ Don't imagine that they want to deal with this alone; give them space but make sure they know you are there for them.

▶ Don't be afraid to talk about the dead person. Just because they are dead doesn't mean they have been erased from a person's memory.

▶ Be prepared for your friend, parent or relative to go through a series of emotional highs and lows – it's all part of the grieving process.

From *Families: Can't Live With Them, Can't Live Without Them!* by Anita Naik

Suicide

'My sister killed herself. She didn't leave a note and we have no idea why she was so unhappy. I love her but it was such a selfish thing to do – she's torn our family apart.' – Kieran, 14

A death by suicide is a confusing and deeply disturbing experience for those left behind. If the deceased left a note you may understand why they saw suicide as the only solution to their problem. If not, you may be left in the dark to wonder why it happened. People who take their own lives do so because they can see no other way out of their troubles. Blaming yourself or thinking 'If only I had done this or said that' is of no use. They died because they wanted to put an end to their suffering and misery, not because they wanted you to feel bad. If someone in your family has killed themselves, it's important for your family to seek counselling. They need to learn to accept what has happened.

From *Families: Can't Live With Them, Can't Live Without Them!* by Anita Naik

In groups

1. Discuss what you learn from Tara's experience about how someone feels when a close friend dies.

2. People often avoid talking about death. Why is death such a taboo subject? Why is it important to talk to someone who has suffered a bereavement?

3. Discuss the advice about how to offer support to someone who has lost a close friend or relative. Draw up a list of Dos and Don'ts on how you can help a friend who has been bereaved.

for your folder

Imagine that you have just changed schools. The brother or sister of a friend from your old school has died. Draft a letter of condolence. Before you put it in your folder, show it to some other members of the class. Which of your letters do you think the person would find the most comforting?

16 Marriage and Partnerships

Why marry?

Marriage **1** The legal union of a man and a woman in order to live together and often to have children **2** an act or ceremony establishing this union **3** an intimate union (*the marriage of true minds*)

> What's the point of getting married when living together is perfectly acceptable?

> I want to remain independent – I don't want to be tied to one person for life.

> I don't see the point of living together – we might just as well get married.

> My boyfriend and I want children, so we think it's better to be married for their sake.

> We want to be together and we want our families and friends to be there when we make a formal commitment.

> Marriage is just a piece of paper we love each other and we want to be together so why do we need some public ceremony?

> I want to get married because that way you can be sure that the other person is going to stay with you.

> I am a Christian, so it's important for me to get married in church. I believe that the promises I make are to God as well as to my partner.

> Marriage is an old-fashioned institution. Why do women change their title and surname when men don't? It's still just a means of enslaving women!

 In groups

1. Talk about the different responses given by the young people above to the question 'Why marry?' Which views do you agree and disagree with?
2. What do you think marriage means for the people involved and for their families and friends?

Marriage vows

In a Church of England marriage service the bride and groom will agree that:

> I, (Name), take you, (Name), to be my wife/husband; to have and to hold; from this day forward; for better, for worse, for richer, for poorer, in sickness and in health, to love, and to cherish, till death us do part, according to God's holy law; and this is my solemn vow.

Couples who want to get married but who don't want a religious ceremony (whether Christian or any other religion) may choose a civil marriage ceremony. In a civil ceremony the only words a couple need to say to each other are:

> I (Name) hereby solemnly declare that I know of no legal impediment to my marrying (Name).
> I call upon these persons here present to witness that I (Name) do take thee (Name) to be my lawful wedded husband/wife.

 In pairs

Discuss these wedding vows.

1. What commitments do the vows made in a Church of England ceremony entail?
2. What commitments do the vows made in a civil ceremony entail?
3. Are these appropriate for a modern marriage?
4. Write your own marriage vows for a civil ceremony.

 In groups

1. Do you think a commitment to marriage made in a religious ceremony makes a difference to the strength of the marriage?
2. Do you think couples should get married in church if they don't believe in God?
3. Should both partners wear wedding rings? Give your reasons.

Living together

Many people decide to live together instead of getting married. This is called **cohabitation**. Some couples cohabit for a short or long period of time before getting married. For other couples, cohabitation is their alternative to marriage.

Why cohabit?

Cohabitation seems a good way to have some of the benefits of marriage while preparing for marriage or, at least, an opportunity for those who do not feel ready for the demands of marriage to enjoy the advantages of sexual co-residence. Couples can learn about each other as they share expenses, and see if the partner makes an acceptable mate. If they prove incompatible, then breaking up seems easy to do, without legal formalities and personal loss.

From Marriage-Lite by Patricia Morgan

Cohabitation – a fragile and short-lived state

The most striking – and most often unappreciated – fact about cohabitation is that it tends to be short-lived. When we hear of cohabitations being 'stable unions', this usually refers to ones producing children. However, less than one in ten British women having their first child in cohabitation are still cohabiting ten years on, or only 8.7 per cent. Just over a third would have married by five years and two-fifths by ten years, but a half will be lone unmarried mothers because their relationships have dissolved.

It may not therefore be surprising that in a survey of cohabitants made in Australia, only 43 per cent felt 'secure' or 'very secure' in their informal relationship, compared to 91 per cent of marrieds. The rest felt insecure – like Pauline, who had lived with David for four and a half years:

'You don't know how long it will last for, even if you do your best to please him. You can't be sure whether there will be a tomorrow with your partner in the first place. … but you have to accept things as they are, I suppose … it affects you in many ways. You cannot plan for the future, you cannot think of buying a car together or a house, to have a child, or even to love him fully, if you know that tomorrow he may not be there.'

Adapted from Marriage-Lite by Patricia Morgan

 In groups

1. What are the advantages and disadvantages of cohabiting instead of getting married?
2. If you cohabited, would you feel that your relationship was fragile and insecure?

Together apart – if you share your lives should you share a home?

Caroline Sullivan asks why more and more couples are choosing to live separately.

Moving in together, setting up home or whatever cosy name you want to give it is, for most of us, a significant marker in the life of a relationship. But according to Jan Trost, a sociologist at the University of Uppsala in Sweden, a growing number of couples are opting out of moving in together. 'Living apart together', as he calls it, is already a recognised phenomenon across Europe. While there are no figures for Britain, the growing number of single-person households – currently 16% in England and Wales, with a projection of almost 50% by 2010 – suggests that many will be committed couples who choose not to share their space.

Living together forces a rearrangement of the mental as well as the physical furniture which some just don't want to negotiate. Living apart together, on the other hand, doesn't necessarily imply lack of commitment, but instead an acknowledgement of boundaries. 'Two people may be mad about each other, but living together doesn't always feel like a natural progression,' observes Karen Frayne, 28, a publisher in a three-year relationship with a co-worker. 'It wouldn't exactly be unbearable being in the same living space, but I want to be able to do exactly what I want, when I want. I want to be financially autonomous and when you're on your own you can prioritise what you do with your money. I don't want to amalgamate personalities.'

From The Guardian

In pairs

'Living apart together' – do you think it's a commitment? Give your reasons.

Arranged marriages

"The practice of arranged marriages is often presented as an explanation for the oppression of Asian girls and for conflict between Asian parents and their daughters. Newspaper stories tell sensational stories of girls forced into marriages against their will, and present Asian girls as torn between two separate lives: one living unhappily at home and another at school envying the greater freedom of their white friends. The stereotypical picture is of a girl caught between two cultures, at home in neither. The stereotype gives a very distorted picture of arranged marriage and hides the wide range of relationships which can exist between an Asian girl and her parents."

From *Speaking Out: Black Girls in Britain* by Audrey Osler

"I have mixed feelings about arranged marriage. The issue for me is not whether or not you should have an arranged marriage but whether you should have choice. There is the question of whether you want to get married at all. To me it seems rather crude that at a certain age they should want you to marry and it should be a certain type of person."

Anita

"The thing about arranged marriage is whether or not you see the person and have a chance to make your own mind up about him. In the past you didn't usually see the person. Now you phone him and he phones you and you get to meet and everything. Before, no one would allow it."

Jasbir

No regrets

Thousands of African, European and Asian women enter into arranged marriages every year. In many cases, it's a success.

It worked for Taz
It certainly worked for 27-year-old Taz Nazir from Bradford. When she turned 19, her parents decided it was time to find her a husband. 'My parents had a very successful arranged marriage and I felt it was the best way,' she says. When her uncle came over from Pakistan, he approached her parents about a cousin he felt would be right for Taz. When the cousin's mother called Taz's father the next day to ask for her hand in marriage for her son, he agreed in principle, but said that the final decision rested with Taz. She explains: 'Before I flew out to Kashmir, my father sat me down and told me that if I didn't feel happy about it, I was to say so and I could come home.' Taz explains that most women who enter into an arranged marriage are asked if they are happy with it, as it states in the Koran that both parties must give their consent to be accepted by Islam.

Nervous
Taz was nervous when she arrived in Kashmir to meet her potential husband. 'He was quite short and needed a good haircut, but other than that I thought he looked nice,' she recalls. 'We didn't talk about why I was there, but my aunt set up a formal meeting at her house a week later. I was really nervous because I didn't know if he would like me. When my aunt ushered him into the room and closed the door, I was really embarrassed and didn't know what to say. After a few formal questions about what I did back home, he asked me if I was being forced into this or if I had a choice and that made me relax. It was clear that he wouldn't be a strict husband and he seemed open-minded and generous which was important to me because I wanted to finish my education back in the UK.'

We just chatted all night
When they married, the pair had never kissed and had had just one conversation about where they would settle down. She laughs when she remembers the wedding night: 'I was so nervous, but my husband could see that, so we just chatted all night.'

Taz has no regrets. She believes she couldn't have found anyone more suitable to herself – and the happy couple now live in Bradford with their two small children. But sadly, many women aren't so lucky. As second-generation Asian, African and Eastern European women become more accustomed to the ways of the West and want to make their own choices, some parents are resorting to force in order to make their children obey their choices. It has been estimated that 1000 young women from the UK are forced into marriages every year. Unlike an arranged marriage a forced marriage is conducted without the valid consent of both parties.

From 'Till Death Do Us Part' by Caitlyn McCarthy

In groups
Discuss what you learn from this page about arranged marriages. Do you think most people have a distorted view of arranged marriage? What is your opinion of the tradition that some cultures have of arranged marriages? How would you feel if your parents or guardians helped to choose a husband or wife for you?

Statistics show that the younger the age of the wife at marriage, the greater the risk of the marriage ending in divorce.

Can your first love last forever?

YES: We were made for each other

Schoolgirl Jane Challand couldn't believe her luck when a good-looking boy asked her to dance at a friend's party.

And the shy 16-year-old jumped at the chance when he suggested going out on a date.

Jane and Chris Aspinall, now both 24, never looked back. Eight years after the fateful meeting, they are still together – and getting married.

Factory worker Chris was Jane's first and only serious relationship. But she doesn't think she's missed out.

She says: 'I think I am the luckiest girl in the world because I met the man of my dreams when I was so young. I know girls who have been out with loads of men because they are desperate to find the right person. I haven't had to go through all that.

'Chris is my soulmate and we are as madly in love with each other now as we were eight years ago. We have so much in common. We laugh at the same things, we have similar personalities and we enjoy the same hobbies.

'Chris and I have grown together in every way – and I could never imagine being with anyone else.'

NO – I grew up but unfortunately he never did

Stacey Lawrence met her childhood sweetheart when she was just 11. She began dating him at 14 and by the age of 16 was talking about marriage.

But within three years she and Danny Stephens had grown apart – both wanting very different things from their lives.

While Stacey decided to go to university, Danny drifted aimlessly from one casual job to the next. Three months ago it was all over.

Art student Stacey says: 'I believed Danny was my soulmate and I never doubted we'd have a future together. For the first year after we left school everything was fine. We had the same friends and did everything together. We were as close as we'd always been. But when I started university everything changed.

'I met lots of people and began to form other interests away from Danny which he resented. I discovered things like going to the theatre and visiting art galleries and exhibitions, but Danny was only interested in going to the pub with his mates. He never felt comfortable with my friends from university.

'I felt Danny was stifling me and trying to stop me from growing up. Soon I realised that the last thing I wanted to do was settle down with Danny and get married.

'It was obvious we had become poles apart. I realised it is hard to stay with

Why do so many teenage marriages fail?

According to Zelda West-Meads, a counsellor for the National Marriage Guidance Council, it's because of the changes we all go through.

'The person you were when you got married at 18 may not be the same person you are at 22. Some people who marry young get to their twenties and find they've developed in different ways and they've no longer got anything in common.'

So even if you seem perfectly suited when you get married, that doesn't mean you'll always seem the same way. And while some couples argue that being together from so early an age helps them to grow together and understand each other more, others find they can't cope with their partner's changing ways.

Zelda also reckons a lot of couples' marriages hit the rocks because they've wed for the wrong reasons. Either the girl's pregnant and they've had to get married (one of the worst starts you can ever get to married life), or all their friends are doing it and it seems like a good idea. Or, worse still, they're doing it to escape from an unhappy home life.

In fact, all the pressures of married life seem to increase when you're young. Says Zelda: 'Young couples tend to be a lot poorer, which creates tension. They may also be living with parents, which puts an intolerable pressure on a relationship.'

A lot depends on you, and how much you feel you're giving up. Says Zelda: 'Some young people find they haven't done enough in terms of going out with different people. They've often been a couple since they were 15 or 16, so they've never really experienced other relationships.'

 In groups

1. Why do you think teenage marriages fail so often?
2. What do you think is the best age for young people to get married?
3. How can you tell if what you feel is enough to base a lifetime commitment on?

for your folder 'It wasn't like I thought it would be.' Write a story about a teenager who finds that married life is very different from their expectations of it.

Becoming a Parent

Being a parent

Being a parent is probably the most difficult and demanding job people ever do. Many parents find it hard to understand what their children need. The more you understand what your child needs, the better you'll be able to carry out your responsibilities as a parent. Here is some advice for new parents from a guide for parents of 0–5 year olds.

Your Baby's Needs

The newborn baby

The world is a strange and terrifying place for a newborn baby. You can help your baby realise that it can also be a friendly, happy place by meeting his needs reasonably soon after they are felt, and by providing lots of cuddles and closeness. Remember, you can't spoil new babies – they have no idea about the world or the needs of others. All they can feel is their own needs.

If your baby cries a lot, it might help to realise that he may be finding it hard to adjust to this new and frightening world.

Crying is your baby's only language. He has no other way of expressing his needs to you. He doesn't know that he is supposed to sleep at night or that it might annoy you when he doesn't. Sooner or later all babies learn these things, but in the meantime it takes a lot of patience and understanding from parents. Often it might need more patience than you feel you've got, especially if you're very tired. If you feel you can't cope with your baby's crying, ask a friend or neighbour to take over, even for an hour. You could also ask your midwife or health visitor for advice or ring the Cry-sis helpline (020 7404 5011).

Remember that:

In the first few months of life a new baby spends on average at least two hours in every 24-hour period crying. So crying is perfectly normal behaviour.

Crying is meant to be a sound which parents find difficult to ignore. That is nature's way of ensuring that the baby's needs will be met.

Crying is neither your fault nor your baby's, and things will get better later on.

The older baby

By the time your baby is a few months old, things will probably be much easier and you will understand much better your baby's needs and routines.

You will notice your baby's personality developing, and the speed at which he develops will often surprise you. Accept that he does things at his own pace – he may do one clever thing very early on, but another quite late, it really doesn't matter. New parents sometimes get upset by comparing their baby's progress to that of other babies they know. All babies, like adults, have their good and bad points, and you will be much happier if your try to accept your own baby as he is.

Learning through play

Playing is an important way babies can practise new skills and learn about the world around them. Only a very unhappy or ill child will not want to play. Through play you can help your child to learn all kinds of new skills, so never feel guilty about spending time playing with your child. However, don't feel you have to join in all the time. Children need to make some of the exciting discoveries for themselves.

Try to make life easier for yourself by moving any dangerous, breakable or valuable objects out of reach, so that your child can explore safely and you can feel more relaxed.

It's never too soon to start reading to your child. Hearing stories helps to improve a young child's listening and language skills.

Provide a variety of toys – a wooden spoon and a plastic cup are just as exciting to your baby as expensive new toys. If you're not sure which toys are right for which age, ask your health visitor or friends with children.

Adapted from 'Putting Children First' and 'Listening to Children', NSPCC

 In pairs

1. What do you learn from the information on this page about a baby's needs?
2. Why do babies cry so much in the first few months of their lives?
3. Why is it wrong to compare your baby with other people's babies?
4. Why is it important to play with very young children?

 For research

Find out about the books that are suitable for reading to very young children. You could each write a review recommending a particular book and produce a class guide – 'Books for Babies'.

What do children need?

Children have three essential types of needs – emotional, physical and intellectual. You may not be able to meet all their needs as successfully as you would like. What matters is doing the best you can.

Love

This is the most vital need of all. If you can love children without expecting anything in return, they will grow up feeling more confident and positive about themselves, and more able to love others.

Praise

Children need a lot of praise – not just for achieving things, but for trying too.

Physical care

This includes warmth, regular nutritious meals and plenty of rest.

Routines

Most children feel more secure if a few things happen at roughly the same time every day, and if any changes in routine are explained to them.

Stimulation

Try to provide a variety of creative, interesting things for your children to do. Encourage them to explore and take on new challenges if you think they are ready for them. Your interest and praise will help to build self-esteem.

Talking

Talk to your baby or child as much as possible and encourage them to talk to you.

Independence

This means encouraging them to learn to do things for themselves, like getting dressed and feeding themselves. It also means allowing them to make choices sometimes, perhaps about which clothes they wear or which toys they prefer to play with.

Respect

Children deserve to be treated with courtesy, just like adults. They should be told about decisions which affect them, like hospital visits or separations. They have rights too.

Dealing with bad behaviour

People have very different ideas about good and bad behaviour. What is acceptable in one family can be quite the opposite in another.

People also have different views on the best way to deal with bad behaviour.

It may seem that shouting loudly, slapping or threatening does the trick more quickly at first, but it will not teach children how to use self-control. Once they get used to angry, loud voices and smacks, you will find it much harder to control them by showing disappointment or disapproval or by using other gentler methods of persuasion.

How to meet your children's needs

- Make time for your children and try to see that all their basic needs are met. Accept that this will mean making sacrifices, especially in the early years.

- Listen to what they have to say, and believe what they tell you.

- Give them lots of love and praise. The first five years are crucial for developing their confidence and self-esteem.

- Establish consistent rules which they should learn to respect, but try not to make too many demands. Decide which rules are the most important for you, and try to be flexible on others. Small children don't easily remember or understand adult rules.

Adapted from 'Putting Children First' and 'Listening to Children', NSPCC

In groups

What do you learn from this page about children's needs? Talk about their different kinds of needs – emotional, physical and intellectual – and what parents should do in order to meet them.

From a report by Peter Foster in the *Daily Telegraph*

Most parents in favour of smacking children

Seven out of ten parents believe it is acceptable to smack their children if they misbehave according to a new survey.

The findings of the ICM poll for BBC Radio 4's *Today* programme give widespread support to the Government's decision to continue to allow parents to smack their children despite lobbying from welfare groups who want it made illegal.

Under current British law a parent has the right to use 'reasonable chastisment' but six other European countries – Sweden, Austria, Cyprus, Denmark, Finland and Norway – have banned all forms of physical punishment against children.

In groups

'I don't agree with smacking. Very little children often don't understand why they've been smacked and older children just resent it. There are much better alternative ways of disciplining children.' Say why you agree or disagree with this view and discuss alternative ways of dealing with bad behaviour.

Feedback

Share your views in a class discussion about how to deal with bad behaviour.

for your folder 'It's not easy being a parent.' Write a short statement saying why you agree or disagree with this view.

Teenage parents

Britain has the highest rate of teenage pregnancy in Europe, five times higher than the rate in the Netherlands. Each year over 90,000 teenagers in Britain become pregnant, resulting in 56,000 babies being born. Ninety percent of teenage births are outside marriage.

" I had my daughter Amy when I was 15. I wasn't planning to have sex and I was definitely not planning to have a baby. I thought it wouldn't happen to me. I love my daughter and would not be without her but if I had my time over again I would wait before having sex. "

Emma, 18-year-old A level student

Being a teenage mother

What is it like to become a mother when you are still a teenager? How does it feel to have another person entirely dependent on you? And when your friends are concerned about things that seem trivial, how do you cope with the way life has changed for you?

I had twins at 13

Donna Dowman describes how the birth of her daughters changed her life.

I went into labour on January 5 1999. It was evening and as I lay on my bed, an agonising pain shot through my stomach. Early next morning my two little girls, Rachel and Rebecca were born.

At first I thought they were the ugliest things I had ever seen. 'Take them away!' I shouted. I couldn't bear them near me. But when I laid eyes on them the next morning, I couldn't help falling in love. They were so tiny and perfect. I felt a sudden urge to love and protect them.

Within days of going home, I came down to earth with a thud. I was completely unprepared for being a mum. It was exhausting. There was no time to have a bath or wash my hair – I was like a zombie. Mum helped, but I was the twins' mum and they were my responsibility.

I wouldn't swap the twins for the world, but part of me wishes they'd come along later, so I could enjoy being a teenager. Money is always short – we survive on Mum's wages – but any spare cash goes on the twins. I can only afford to buy things like CDs and make-up once in a blue moon and holidays are out of the question.

Even though times are tough, I'm determined to make something of my life. I'm going back to college to take my GCSEs when the twins are older and I don't see my life as being over any more.

Adapted from an article in Sugar

In groups

1. What problems did Donna face after the arrival of her babies?
2. What helped Donna to cope?
3. List all the ways that life changes for a girl who becomes a mother while she is still at school.
4. Do you think a 13-year-old can be a good mother? Give your reasons.

Boys to pay for teen pregnancy

The Child Support Agency is to be ordered to make it a priority to pursue the fathers of babies born to teenage girls, under a drive to halve Britain's high rate of teenage pregnancy.

The government wants young men to be made painfully aware that fathering children could cost them up to a quarter of their income for 18 years. The Child Support Agency will be told to track down the fathers of babies born to teenagers, regardless of their ability to pay maintenance. Just 15% of teenage mothers receive any child maintenance and ministers want the fathers to pay up. Even if they are without a job, they will be made to pay 5 pounds a week.

Parenting and sexual health classes are, meanwhile, to be made compulsory in all young offender institutions, following the discovery that up to a third of their 11,000 male inmates have fathered children.

The measures reflect a shift from the idea that the teenage pregnancy rate can be reduced by focusing overwhelmingly on girls.

Ministers intend the package to be seen as firm but fair. They have already let it be known that they want local authorities to stop placing teenage mothers in council flats. If they cannot live with either their parents or their partner, they want teenage mothers to be placed in supervised hostels run by social services.

Under a pilot scheme 'pregnancy advisers' will be appointed in some parts of the country to give pregnant teenagers impartial information on adoption, abortion and keeping the baby.

One reason for trying out the advisers – NHS workers such as health visitors or community nurses – is that teenagers may feel more willing to approach them than their family doctor.

Achieving the target of a 50% cut in conceptions among under 18s by 2010 would bring Britain in line with other European countries, which have achieved comparable reductions with

Adapted from a report by David Brindle in The Guardian

In groups

Discuss the measures that the government is introducing to try to halve the number of teenage pregnancies.

1. Are they fair? In particular, **a)** Should the Child Support Agency force teenage fathers to pay maintenance? **b)** Should teenage mothers be placed in supervised hostels rather than council flats?
2. Do you think the measures will be effective? Can you suggest any other measures that you think would be more effective?

Feedback

Share your ideas on how to cut the teenage pregnancy rate in a class debate.

Teenage fathers

Many teenage mothers do not continue to have a relationship with the father of their child, after the baby is born. For the teenage father who wants to stay involved with his child there are often insurmountable obstacles.

Adapted from an article by Maureen Freely in *The Guardian*

Hurdles for the teenage father

There is, first of all, the question of access. It will be the mother who decides when he can see his child. If he thinks she is being unfair, there won't be much he can do. Her parents are likely to be strong influences on her decisions, he won't be able to do much about that either. Then there is the question of accommodation. The underage father is not likely to receive special treatment in the housing office. If his lodgings are not suitable for children, then what?

If teenage fathers aren't involved with their children, it can be due to the difficulties of staying in touch, rather than a lack of will, as a survey of forty young fathers showed. Asked what he thought fathers should do or be, one said, 'You've just got to be there for them, just be there if they need you.' Another said, 'It's about being there for them. My Dad were never there.' A third said,'When you've got both like a Mam and a Dad, then they [children] see two sides, don't they? That's got to be better, two points of view about stuff.' A fourth said, 'Bairns got to know they're loved – wanted, like. I'd not want my son to grow up thinking he weren't wanted 'cause I didn't see him.' About three-quarters of the fathers thought there was no reason why childcare had to be the sole responsibility of mothers.

In groups

Discuss the difficulties that teenage fathers have of keeping in contact with their children. How important do you think it is for young fathers to keep in contact with their children?

Marriage before fatherhood, say schoolboys

More boys than girls believe they should marry before having children, according to a survey for a new children's magazine.

While 84% of 13 year old boys want to be married before they become fathers, only 52% of girls think they should marry before motherhood.

The survey of 1500 children was conducted for the new monthly magazine *Newspaper*.

Hayley Hobbs, co-founder of the *Newspaper*, said: 'The results were surprising. A huge percentage of 13 year old boys want to be married before they have children. And they appear to be very sensible – we received a lot of thoughtful comments.

'The girls were saying they did not see it as important. Overall 73 per cent wanted to get married at some point but only 10 per cent thought it would be in their teens. Ninety per cent thought it would be in their twenties.

Mostly their reasons were based on their own experiences, their parents' experiences and those of friends around them. They all felt long-standing relationships were very important whether they believed in marriage or not.'

Adapted from a report by Catherine Elsworth in the *Sunday Telegraph*

In groups

Discuss the findings of the survey (see article, above). Do they surprise you? Do you think it's important to be married before you have children? Is there a difference in the views of the boys and girls in your group?

Shotgun marriages

In the past, a young man who got a young girl pregnant was expected 'to do the decent thing' and marry her. A marriage which occurred because pressure was put on a young man to marry his pregnant girlfriend was called a 'shotgun wedding'.

In groups

What do you think of 'shotgun weddings'? Should there be social pressure on a young couple to get married if the girl is pregnant? Would getting married force young fathers to take more responsibility for their children?

In pairs

Imagine you work for a company which makes television programmes. You have been asked to submit an outline for a documentary on the subject of teenage pregnancies and teenage parents. Draft your proposal, making clear the points that you would want the programme to make about the government's proposals and about the problems faced by young mothers and young fathers.

for your folder

Write a poem or a story expressing the thoughts and feelings of either a teenage mother or a teenage father.

18

Social and Moral Dilemmas – Where Do You Stand?

Abortion

If a woman becomes pregnant, she has three choices. She can choose to have the baby and look after it herself, have the baby and put it forward for adoption or have an abortion.

The right to choose – arguments for abortion

- 'It's my body, therefore it should be up to me to decide what I want to do.'
- 'I believe that all human life is of value. But quality of life matters. You should be able to choose whether or not it's right for you to bring another person into the world and a lot will depend on your circumstances at the time.'
- 'If abortion wasn't available legally, you'd go back to the bad old days when thousands of women had "back-street abortions" in which they put themselves at risk.'
- 'It's more responsible to have an abortion if you get pregnant when you're very young and not in a position to be able to support a baby or offer it a home.'

The right to life – arguments against abortion

- 'It is wrong to suggest that human life begins at birth. I believe that it begins at conception. So anyone who has an abortion is taking a human life. It's the equivalent of murder.'
- 'The widespread practice of abortion has lowered the value of human life. Abortion should be illegal.'
- 'People talk about women's rights but what about the rights of the unborn baby? It has a right to life.'
- 'The availability of abortion means that people are more promiscuous than they would otherwise be. If abortion weren't so easy, then people would think more carefully about when it's right to have sex.'

⊕ In groups

Discuss these views on abortion. Are all abortions morally wrong? Should women have the right to choose?

Share your views and work together to produce a statement which summarizes the different opinions of the members of your group.

？ For research

Choose a spokesperson from each group to read their group's statement and discuss your views in a class discussion.

GPs back reform of abortion law

Most GPs think the law should be changed to allow women easier abortions within the first three months, without having to get the written consent of two doctors, according to a survey from the family planning organisation, Marie Stopes International.

The vast majority of the 8000 GPs contacted for the survey (82%) said they were 'broadly pro-choice' and 60% supported changing the law so that a woman's request to a doctor in the first trimester (14 weeks) for an abortion would suffice.

Most doctors (84%) said they thought a GP who had a conscientious objection to an abortion should be obliged to declare it to a woman who wanted a termination. But 10% of GPs did not agree. Of the 118 doctors answering the question who said they were anti-abortion, nearly 27% thought they should not have to tell the woman of their convictions.

Helen Axby of Marie Stopes International said the report showed abortion in Britain today was 'a complete lottery – arbitrary, discriminatory and unfair. At the moment the woman is at the mercy of two doctors exercising discretionary powers.

'We are disturbed by the finding that a small, but significant minority, of GPs may be imposing their own moral standards and values upon women, causing distress, delay and financial

The law on abortion

In Europe, the law varies from country to country. In England, Scotland and Wales an abortion is legal if it is carried out for one or more of the following reasons:

1. The mother's life is at risk.
2. There is a greater risk to the physical or mental health of the pregnant woman than if the pregnancy is terminated.
3. To continue the pregnancy would involve greater risk to the physical or mental health of the existing children of the pregnant woman than if it were terminated.
4. There is a substantial risk that the child would be born with a serious physical or mental abnormality.

Abortions are not permitted after 24 weeks of pregnancy except in cases of foetal handicap or risk to the life of the mother.

⊕ In groups

1. Should doctors have the final decision on whether or not a woman has an abortion? Should doctors who are anti-abortion have to tell a woman who is seeking an abortion what they believe?
2. Discuss your views on the abortion laws. Do you think they need reforming?
3. Should abortion be available on demand during the first 14 weeks of pregnancy?

Adapted from an article by Sarah Boseley in *The Guardian*

Abortion Factfile

> In 1998 177,332 abortions were performed in England and Wales.

> One in four women will have a termination.

> A quarter of women who have abortions are aged between 20 and 24.

> Almost 90% of abortions take place in the first twelve weeks of pregnancy.

> A Mori poll in 1997 found that 67 per cent of women believe 'Abortion should be made legally available for all who want it.'

> In 1997 almost 10,000 women travelled to England to have an abortion. Most came from other parts of the British Isles where abortion is illegal or restricted, such as the Irish Republic.

> Abortions are not automatically available on the NHS, but on average the NHS pays for about 74 per cent of terminations.

From an article by Katie Aston in 19 Special Report: Abortion © 19/IPC Syndication

'The only choice for me'

Claire Cottle, a 20-year-old student from London, explains why she decided to have an abortion

'I'd just split up with a guy I'd been seeing for a few weeks at university when I discovered I was pregnant. I was devastated. I had my finals coming up and I just knew I wasn't ready for a baby. I always thought we'd been careful, but a condom must have split without us knowing. I knew my parents would go mad so I only told my best mate.

I take the decision to have kids very seriously and when I decide to start a family, I want it to be at the right time – when I feel I'm mature enough and can offer a stable and financially secure home. I believe that if I had had the baby, it would have ruined not only my own life and any chance of a career, but the baby's life, too.

I contacted the British Pregnancy Advisory Service. They were really supportive and immediately booked me in for my initial consultation with a doctor and a counsellor. The woman I met was lovely – not at all judgmental as I'd feared. We talked through all the options, including adoption and bringing up the baby myself. There was no pressure, but she asked me lots of questions to make sure I was certain I wanted a termination. A doctor examined me and I was booked in for an early medical abortion the following week at the cost of £300. I didn't even ask about having it done on the NHS – I just wanted it over quickly, and I used some of my student loan to pay for it.

I was only five weeks pregnant when I had the termination, so I didn't think of it as a baby at all. If I hadn't been able to have an abortion here, I would have found the money to travel abroad. There's no way I would have gone through with it, no matter what anyone said.'

From an article by Katie Aston in 19 Special Report: Abortion

> I don't know what people feel like when they get an abortion. I've never had one, and never want to have one. But I think in a way, it's a bad way to get rid of a child. Because you have the chance of life, your mum could have just said no. They gave you the chance for life, and you've had a chance to have a life so you should give that baby one chance.

***Teenage Pregnancy*, report by the Social Exclusion Unit**

In pairs

1. Do you agree with what the young woman says about abortion in the quote above?

2. Do you think the father of an unborn baby has any right to have a say in whether or not a woman has an abortion?

3. Either role play or write the script for a scene in which a teenage girl who is pregnant confides in someone they trust and together they discuss the options open to her.

for your folder

1 Imagine that you work for a teenage magazine, answering letters sent to Dear Carrie. Write your reply to Tony's letter.

Dear Carrie
My girlfriend's 15. When she told me she was pregnant I was thrilled she was going to have my baby. Now she tells me she's going to have an abortion. She says we're too young to be parents and that it wouldn't be fair on the baby to bring it into the world. But I know she'd be a great mum. She's got a little sister and she's ever so good with her. I was planning to stay on at school, but I've told her I'd leave and get a job to support the baby. But she says she's determined she's not going to have it. What should I do? – Tony, 16

2 Write a statement in which you give your views on the issue of abortion.

In groups

1. Discuss the reasons why Claire Cottle chose to have an abortion (above). Do you think they were good reasons? Were any of her reasons selfish ones?

2. What do you learn from Claire Cottle's experience about all the things a woman has to consider when making the decision whether or not to have an abortion?

Genetic engineering

Genetic engineering is the term used to describe the techniques whereby certain characteristics of an animal or plant are changed by transferring genes from one organism to another, or by changing genetic material within an organism.

Supporters claim that the benefits of genetic engineering outweigh the risks. Opponents argue that not only are we unsure what the consequences may be, but that tampering with nature is ethically wrong.

A slippery slope?

This is yet another step on the slippery slope to designer babies. It is science out of control and at its most irresponsible. People should wake up to the fact that genetic engineering of people could be just around the corner.

Dave King, a campaigner against human genetic engineering, commenting on the news that scientists had created ANDi

Scientists create first genetically modified monkey

Scientists have created the world's first genetically modified monkey, a baby rhesus called ANDi.

The feat could hasten the development of new treatments for a range of diseases, from diabetes and breast cancer to Parkinson's and HIV. 'It's a special step, said the head of the American team, Professor Gerald Schatten. 'We're at an extraordinary moment in the history of humans.'

But anit-vivisectionists fear that ANDi, who was born on Oct 2 2000, will herald a surge in experiments on monkeys. They condemned the research as 'abhorrent' and accused Prof Schatten of 'playing God'.

The work also raises the issue of whether similar techniques could be used to create GM humans.

ANDi – the name is 'inserted DNA' spelt backwards – received an extra marker gene, from a jellyfish, while he was still an unfertilised egg, making him the world's first genetically modified non-human primate.

The technique used to make ANDi could pave the way to the creation of laboratory monkeys that carry human genes, offering the opportunity for medical researchers to make more realistic models of human disease.

'We could just as easily introduce, for example, an Alzheimer's gene, to accelerate the development of a vaccine for that disease,' said Professor Schatten.

'Monkeys like ANDi will quickly but safely help us to determine if innovative therapies are safe and effective.'

The advance was attacked by the British Union for the Abolition of Vivisection because it would lead to more experiments on monkeys.

The campaign director, Wendy Higgins, said: 'It's shocking that this should happen at a time when there are worldwide calls to reduce or even abolish research using primates.'

Sue Mayer, of the pressure group GeneWatch, said it was also concerned by ANDi. 'It's incredibly important that we take stock and don't allow it to lead to enormous animal suffering that isn't justified.'

Adapted from the *Daily Telegraph*

In groups

Discuss these questions.

1. Is the genetic modification of animals in general, and primates (the higher mammals) in particular, morally justifiable?

2. Will such research inevitably be extended to humans and, if so, would that be wrong?

3. What unforeseen consequences might there be if animal species are modified on a large scale?

4. Is the genetic modification of animals compatible with our duty as custodians of the animal kingdom?

Cloning

Cloning is the term used to describe the process in which a cell taken from an animal is used to produce another animal identical to the one from which the donor cell was taken. In 1997, scientists in Edinburgh announced that they had succeeded for the first time in producing a clone of an adult animal, a sheep called Dolly.

The achievement was hailed by some people as a breakthrough on the grounds that it could increase our understanding of the ageing process and might also lead to the production of cheaper and more effective medicines. Others were less enthusiastic, arguing that it raised the spectre of cloned human beings and that the development has ethical implications which called into question the desirability of all forms of genetic engineering.

In groups

1. What are the arguments for and against human cloning?

2. 'Human cloning is inevitable. But it must be strictly controlled.' Say why you agree or disagree with this statement.

Genetically modified foods

Over the past two decades, it has become possible to genetically modify crops, producing, for example, soya beans that are resistant to weedkiller. However, the development of such genetically altered foods has caused a great deal of controversy.

Activists from Earth First demonstrating at a GM crop trial site in Scotland

GM foods – do the benefits outweigh the risks?

Not everyone is happy with the idea of genetically-engineered food, and some people say that the risks are greater than the benefits.

Take the soya for example. Who benefits from the production of these new, engineered crops? In one sense we all do. Certainly the companies which come up with the new crops make money by selling them to the farmer. The farmer also stands to make more money by improving the harvest. And an increased supply of food might also benefit you and me, by lowering food prices in the shops.

But other people are concerned about the possible environmental impact of these genetically-engineered plants. They argue that plants made resistant to weedkillers might breed with the wild relatives of the soya to create new varieties of superweeds – potentially resistant to all man-made weedkillers. These superweeds would spread like wildfire through the countryside, taking over from rarer plants which would become extinct.

However, some of the newly engineered agricultural products might help out the environment. Fruit and vegetables have already been designed that are resistant to insect pests and certain types of disease, and so one day, environmentally dangerous chemicals like pesticides may be unnecessary.

One particular example is a potato which has been genetically engineered to commit suicide when it is infected by a disease-causing fungus. The gene is only switched on when the fungus attacks. The potato dies, but in a field of potatoes this is good news, because the disease is prevented from spreading – without the need for pesticides.

Maybe preservatives could also disappear if we could design food which didn't go off. Far-fetched? Maybe not. Supermarkets already sell a brand of tomato puree which uses tomatoes made resistant to bruising through genetic engineering.

It might sound too good to be true. Indeed, there are fears that by creating super-resistant crops, the disease-causing organisms might one day mutate to overcome these new obstacles and become even more dangerous than they were to start with.

Could genetically-engineered food help the hungry? In places like India and Pakistan, much of the soil is too salty to grow crops. But it might be possible to put a gene from a native salt-loving plant into a food crop like wheat, so that it could be grown in salty soils. Again this sounds like a good idea. But environmental organisations like Greenpeace have argued that poverty, not lack of food, is the reason why people are starving in the Third World. Are the claims made by genetic engineering companies just propaganda?

From What's the Big Idea? Genetics by Martin Brookes

Is GM food dangerous?

Many theoretical risks exist. When scientists insert a foreign gene into an organism this causes it to produce an abnormal substance, which might trigger allergies or could even poison you. But, just as with all food production, those containing harmful substances should be banned by normal regulatory procedures.

There are also fears that the act of genetic modification itself could be harmful, because of various other substances used to squeeze in the gene and switch it on. Another objection is that the foreign gene could interact with the genes that are naturally present, with unknown effects.

As for the foreign gene itself, we eat DNA all the time so there is no general reason why an introduced gene should cause harm. DNA is rapidly broken down in the stomach and by cooking. That is why there is little concern that sugar refined from sugar beet modified to resist insects will cause problems.

From the Daily Telegraph

GM food gets clean bill of health

Eating genetically modified food has yet to be shown to cause the slightest harm to human health anywhere in the world, an international conference has concluded.

'So far, so good,' said Professor Sir John Krebs, chairman of the Organisation on Economic Co-operation and Development conference, of GM food's first decade.

However, Professor Krebs saw a need for improved and continued testing of GM varieties and continual monitoring of the people who ate them.

Adapted from the Daily Telegraph

⊕ In groups

What are the arguments for and against the development of GM foods? Do you think we should continue to develop them, or is the danger that they may cause damage to the environment too great a risk to take?

for your folder Write a short statement expressing your views on GM foods.

Euthanasia – *for* and *against*

The word 'euthanasia' comes from the Greek words 'eu' and 'thanatos', which together mean 'a good death'. Today, the meaning of 'euthanasia' has widened, to include how that good death is brought about. Specifically, 'euthanasia' is understood to mean a good death brought about by a doctor providing drugs or an injection to bring a peaceful end to the dying process.

The case for

The Voluntary Euthanasia Society's aim is to make it legal for a competent adult, who is suffering unbearably from an incurable illness, to receive medical help to die at their own considered and persistent request.

The right to decide

We believe that everyone has the right to choose how they live and die. Each person has value and is worthy of respect, has basic rights and freedoms and the power to control his or her own destiny. Our campaign to legalise assisted dying within certain strictly defined circumstances is fundamentally about *choice*.

Passive euthanasia versus active euthanasia

At the moment, doctors can legally practice 'passive' euthanasia – that is, taking away or withholding treatment even if the person will die. However, doctors cannot directly help the person to die, for example, by giving a lethal injection. We argue that, in situations where a competent terminally ill patient is asking for help to die, passive euthanasia has exactly the same moral and practical result as giving a lethal injection at the patient's request.

Quality of life – pain is not the only issue

Not everyone dies well. At least 5% of terminal pain cannot be fully controlled, even with the best care. Other distressing symptoms such as sickness, incontinence and breathlessness cannot always be relieved.

But pain is not the only issue in decisions about the end of life. What a patient thinks about their quality of life is often far more important. Many people do not want to spend the last days or weeks of their life in a way which, *to them*, is undignified.

Having the power to take control over their life and death can help people to keep a measure of human dignity in the face of their suffering.

The case against

Only God can give and take away life

Some people believe that life is sacred and that no one has the right to purposely take a life. Many religious people follow this principle, so do not agree with suicide and assisted dying. However, there are many religious people who do support voluntary euthanasia, such as Lord Soper, an important Methodist minister who was vice-president of the Voluntary Euthanasia Society. In the Netherlands, Catholic or Dutch Reformed clergymen may be present at assisted deaths. It must also be remembered that religious arguments cannot, and should not, apply to anyone who does not share that religious belief.

The slippery slope – voluntary euthanasia will soon lead to involuntary euthanasia

This argument states that once we have made voluntary euthanasia legal, society will soon allow involuntary euthanasia. This is based on the idea that if we change the law to allow a person to help somebody to die, we will not be able to control it. This is misleading and inaccurate – voluntary euthanasia is based on the right to choose for yourself. It is totally different from murder. There is no evidence to suggest that strictly controlled voluntary euthanasia would inevitably lead to the killing of the sick or elderly against their will.

It will have a damaging effect on society

Some people who do not agree with voluntary euthanasia argue that if it was legalised, it would damage the moral and social foundation of society by removing the traditional principle that man should not kill, and reduce the respect for human life. However, the idea that we should not kill is not absolute, even for those with religious beliefs – killing in war or self-defence is justified by most. We already let people die because they are allowed to refuse treatment which could save their life, and this has not damaged anyone's respect for the worth of human life.

In Holland, voluntary euthanasia is legally permitted. Yet as the report (below) shows not everyone feels happy about the situation.

Dutch carry 'declaration of life' cards

While the majority of doctors and public opinion in Holland support the practice of voluntary euthanasia, there is growing concern that assisted suicide is increasingly dominating medial practice to the exclusion of other treatments.

More than 10,000 people in Holland have started carrying anti-euthanasia 'passports' because they are frightened of being killed prematurely by over-enthusiastic doctors if they fall ill.

The 'declaration of life' cards, which are being distributed by pro-life groups throughout Holland, carry the words: 'I request that no medical treatment be withheld on the grounds that the future quality of my life will be diminished, because I believe that this is not something that human beings can judge. I request that under no circumstances a life-ending treatment be administered because I am of the opinion that people do not have the right to end life.'

Adapted from an article by Rachel Bridge in the *Daily Telegraph*

⊕ In groups

Imagine that the government is planning to introduce a law legalising voluntary euthanasia. Say why you would be for or against such a law.

From factsheets produced by the Voluntary Euthanasia Society

Living wills – for and against

The living will (also known as an 'advance directive') allows people to leave instructions about their possible medical treatment, in case there comes a time when they are no longer capable of making decisions or of communicating them.

Many people fear that, if they become ill, they could face a situation where they may be given too much treatment when there is little or no chance of recovery, or given treatment which would leave them in a condition they could not cope with. A living will can show that in the future, under clearly defined circumstances, the patient does not want treatment which will help him or her to live longer, such as antibiotics, tube feeding or being kept alive indefinitely on a life support machine.

Pros and cons

The pros of making such a decision are obvious. There would be a chance to extend your freedom of action into that part of your life when you will be unable to express yourself. The chance to remove from your nearest and dearest the dreadful burden of having to decide whether or not life support systems should be used for you. And, not a negligible point, the removal from doctors of the risk of being sued by over-enthusiastic relations after your death if they think treatment should have been more vigorous.

But there are cons too. Could older ailing people be pressured by relations impatient for inheritances to make such wills when they do not want to? Could a cash-strapped NHS seize on their existence as an excuse to stop investing any more money in the care of the very ill and, above all, the elderly? And in purely practical terms, suppose the will you make this year isn't needed for another five or ten years, by which time there is a cure for the conditions you currently fear?

Then there is the religious aspect; what of those people who believe that it is up to their God to decide when and how they die, and that doctors are simply his agents, who must preserve life at all costs? What of those who see the acceptance of living wills as a 'slippery slope' that leads to voluntary euthanasia and ultimately to Hitlerite state-directed culling of unwanted expensively sick people?

From *Living Wills*, the Voluntary Euthanasia Society, and an article by Claire Raynor in the *Sunday Times*

In groups

Discuss the arguments for and against living wills. Which arguments do you find most persuasive? Would you consider making a living will? If so, what would you request in it?

Passive euthanasia – who should decide?

Passive euthanasia is the term used to describe bringing an end to the life of a patient who is incapable of making their own request, such as a person who has been in a coma for several years, for example by switching off their life support machine.

In such cases, the issue is who should take any decision? Should the decision be taken by doctors, on medical grounds only, once they are convinced that everything that could be done for the patient has been done and that there is absolutely no hope of any recovery? Or should any decisions be made by the individual's closest relative or relatives, based on what they feel would have been the patient's wishes?

Or are decisions about ending life too important to leave to doctors or individual relatives? Should it be up to the courts to make decisions in each case according to its particular circumstances?

In groups

Who do you think should make decisions on behalf of patients who are unable to make their own decisions, such as people in a deep and indefinite coma?

Mercy killing or murder?

A Northumbrian doctor, Dr David Moor, was in the headlines in 1999 when he was acquitted of a charge of murder by a jury. Dr Moor was accused of assisting an 85-year-old patient to die. The patient, George Liddell, was in severe agony with terminal bowel cancer. At the trial Dr Moor claimed he was only helping relieve Mr Liddell from his acute pain. Before her father's death Mr Liddell's daughter had long discussions with Dr Moor about her father's condition and publicly defended the doctor's actions.

Although doctor-assisted deaths are unlawful in the UK, surveys show that doctors are willing to help patients who have incurable diseases or are in immense pain to die. A British Medical Association survey in 1994 found that six out of ten doctors had received requests from patients to hasten their deaths and that a third of them had done what the patient asked. A 1998 survey for the *Sunday Times* suggested one in seven GPs admitted assisting patients to die.

for your folder 'Mercy killing or murder?' Write a statement expressing your views on euthanasia and of the fact that, while euthanasia remains illegal, many doctors nevertheless admit having assisted patients, who wished to do so, to die.

19

Standing up for Your Beliefs

Challenging offensive behaviour

From Racism *by Jagdish Gundara and Roger Hewitt*

Racial harassment

In Britain, racial harassment and even assault are frequently experienced by children and young people. Sometimes this takes the form of racist name-calling, sometimes it is more physical.

There have even been racist murders perpetrated against ethnic minority pupils. Although these have mainly been perpetrated against black and Asian young people, racially motivated attacks on whites are not unknown, though rare. It is mainly the black and ethnic minority communities that have come to live in fear of violent attack, so that much smaller instances of harassment, like name calling, come to cause a high level of anxiety. Sometimes racist grafitti is deliberately used to create this atmosphere of uncertainty and terror.

When I came to this country I thought everything would be good and fine but when I went to school everyone was being racist to me. Some of them would say, 'Hey, Hamed, why are you black? I know why you're black. It's because you never had a wash since you were born.' And they say to me, 'You black bastard, what are you doing in this country? You should go back where you came from.'

Hamed, a teenage refugee from Somalia

I gave birth to my daughter – and my daughter's of mixed race – to prove the fact that we can love each other in this world and we can all get on together. But it's hard … My daughter had her nose broken, then they started throwing broken bottles at her. Now she suffers racism from children from eight to fourteen … and we live in fear.

A (white) mother

My mum is from the Philippines and my dad's English. But people are not interested in that and show their ignorance by calling me 'chinky' at school, and going on about slanting eyes. I wish that everyone was like my mum and dad. They love each other even though they come from totally different backgrounds and cultures.

Tom, 14, Edinburgh

 In groups

1. The challenge is to educate the minority of young people who are guilty of racial harassment. How do you think this could be done?

2. Has your school got any special rules about racist bullying? If so, what are they? Either suggest ways of improving them to make them more effective, or, if the school does not have any special rules, suggest what rules it should introduce.

Standing up against racism

From Racism *by Jagdish Gundara and Roger Hewitt*

Racism is both suffered and fought by people every day in very ordinary situations. All of us can speak out against racist behaviour when we see it happening – whether or not we are on the receiving end of it. When we hear racist jokes, when we find that we or our friends are being treated differently because of 'race' or ethnicity, when we see a piece of journalism in the newspaper that we think perpetuates some ethnic stereotype, we can make our views known. Even such apparently small ways can help to fight racism.

In groups

Study the views below and say why you agree or disagree with them.

'It's all very well to say that you should report all acts of racism, but what if you live in an area where there are lots of racists and they go round in gangs? You could end up getting picked on yourself.'

'Racists are just ignorant bullies. The best thing to do is to ignore them. If you take no notice, they'll eventually stop bothering you.'

'It's everybody's responsibility to stamp out racism. If you overhear a racist remark and don't challenge it you're condoning racism.'

'The only way to eradicate racism is through community action, so that acts of racism are exposed and those who perpetrate it are made to apologise and feel ashamed of what they have done.'

for your folder Write an article for a teenage magazine: 'Why we must all stand up against racism'.

Sexual harassment

Sexual harassment is unwanted pestering of a sexual nature and includes physical harassment (such as touching people up), following people, name calling of a sexual nature, whistling etc. It is very common amongst adults and has recently been in the news especially in the form of sexual harassment of women by their bosses at work and women being 'stalked' by men. It also appears to happen a lot amongst young people in and out of school and mainly, but not only, consists of boys harassing girls.

Sexual harassment can be very distressing for the victim but it is often not taken seriously by young people. Young people have a responsibility to not harass other people and to act to stop other people doing it. Too often people think it is 'just a laugh' and do not realise the misery it can cause. Victims of sexual harassment may become anxious and depressed, may feel they cannot go out or to school and may live in fear. In some cases sexual harassment has been a factor in suicide attempts.

These boys kept going on at me about my big breasts. Some of the girls joined in as well. It went on and on. At break. In the corridor. Even in lessons they would send me nasty notes. It got so I didn't want to go to school at all. **14-year-old girl**

From *Sex Matters* by Julian Cohen

In groups

1. 'I think people who wolf-whistle and make crude jokes about women and their bodies are pathetic and immature.' Discuss this view.

2. Make a list of all the different types of behaviour which you think are examples of sexual harassment. Are some forms of sexual harassment more serious than others?

3. How does your school deal with incidents of sexual harassment? Is there a clear policy statement which makes it clear that sexual harassment will not be tolerated? Discuss the school's policy and, if appropriate, suggest any alterations which you think would make the existing policy more effective. If there is no such policy, draft a statement for consideration by the school council.

Should offensive pop songs be censored?

In December 2000 the 26-year-old US rapper Eminem topped the UK charts with his hit single Stan. But critics argue that his songs with their violent, sexist lyrics should be banned.

Eminem's songs have attracted strong criticism from people appalled at their violent content directed at women and gay people. They point to the repeated references to women as 'bitches and hos', especially in the extremely violent song Kim (about his wife). And critics remain unimpressed by the idea that songs such as Role Model are meant to be ironic:

> *Follow me and do exactly what the song says:*
> *Smoke weed, take pills, drop outta school, kill people and drink.*

Once a song is out there, there is no knowing how people are going to understand it.

In interviews Eminem acknowledges the power he has 'to push his fans' buttons' but he assumes they will not take the songs too seriously. Stan – a song featuring a crazed fan, suicide and murder – suggests Eminem wants to put his more deluded fans straight about the importance they should place on his lyrics.

But does the possibility that a song could encourage violence prove the need for censorship? No, say defenders of free speech. If the authorities ban Eminem today, what's to stop them banning anything else they don't like tomorrow?

Those who bought Stan on CD can hear the screams of the girlfriend as the deranged Stan drives off the bridge. On the radio these are censored, as is the swearing – but should they be?

Adapted from 'Eminem – should he be censored?', *The Guardian*

In groups

'Eminem's songs should be banned because the lyrics are offensive to women and gay people.'

'Eminem's songs should be censored because they are full of foul language which many people find offensive.'

'Eminem's lyrics can be misinterpreted and might lead some people to act violently, so his songs should be banned.'

'People are making a fuss over nothing. All Eminem's fans know that his lyrics aren't to be taken literally.'

'If you start censoring songs because of their lyrics, who knows what they'll ban. They might ban Bob the Builder, on the grounds that it should be Betty the Builder.'

Discuss these views, saying whether or not you find Eminem's lyrics offensive and whether or not you think his songs should be censored.

What do you do when you feel strongly about a national or international issue? You will often want to make your views known to others. You may want to see some changes in the way people think or behave with regard to particular problems. You may also want to see changes in the way organisations work, or even in the law.

Some people are prepared to risk imprisonment in order to bring their views to the attention of the public because they are so strongly convinced that change needs to happen. History is full of examples of individuals who have had to fight for what they believe – people who could not tolerate injustices and who worked to make the world a fairer place. There are stories of people who challenged systems, organisations and those in authority in order to change things for the better; stories of people who put up with difficulties, barriers, opposition – and of people who wouldn't take 'no' for an answer.

James Mawdsley on his release from a Burmese jail last year. He is committed to campaigning for human rights and democracy in Burma which has a repressive government. During his visit he was sentenced to 17 years hard labour for distributing pro-democracy leaflets. International pressure led to him being deported after spending 411 days in jail but he remains determined to continue even after enduring torture and solitary confinement.

For research

1. Find out about the life story of one individual who changed the world – or part of it! – for the better.

2. Select three 'defining moments' from this person's life which show the person's commitments and values.

3. Choose one area of concern such as the environment, animal cruelty, hunting, children's rights, cruelty to children. Find out about the work of organisations which are involved in campaigning to bring this issue to the attention of the public.

Grandmother has her day in court

by Kirsty Scott

When retired teacher Joan Meredith wanted to make a point about nuclear weapons she sat down in the roadway outside the Trident submarine base on the Clyde.

Yesterday magistrates responded in kind, ordering her to find a comfortable spot in their courtroom and sit for the entire day's proceedings as punishment for non-payment of a £100 fine.

Mrs Meredith, 70, from Northumberland, had been expecting to spend a week in jail for refusing to pay the fine imposed after a peace protest at the Faslane base. She even packed a case for a spell in Low Newton prison near Durham. But magistrates in Alnwick chose to enact a little used section of the Magistrates Court Act and told her she must stay put in the court precincts for the day.

Dressed in a purple T-shirt and matching socks, Mrs Meredith sat at the back of the court listening to proceedings and pronouncing herself satisfied with her sentence.

'I have been sitting on a bench at the back listening with interest to a number of people who did not pay their poll tax and some driving offences. I have found the day quite enlightening. At one stage I was even given a cup of coffee and I must say I have been treated very nicely.'

Mrs Meredith, a grandmother of six, was originally fined after joining a blockade of Faslane organised by the Trident Ploughshares group. A week-long jail term imposed in June was suspended to give her another chance to pay. Mrs Meredith refused to do so because she does not believe her protest was morally wrong.

She would go to more protests, she said yesterday. 'I can't see this making any difference.'

From The Guardian

In pairs

1. Discuss your responses to the article above. Do you think Mrs Meredith was in the right in carrying out her peaceful protest or not? Give reasons for your answer.

2. Do you think the penalty imposed on Mrs Meredith was fair?

3. Talk about whether there are any issues you feel so strongly about that you would risk imprisonment for them.

Violent protest

Some protesters are prepared to damage property, or even to target people, in order to protest against behaviour which they see as wrong. In extreme cases, activists have sent people letter bombs in order to protest and draw attention to their cause.

Animal rights gang sends victim a nail-bomb

MI5 has been called in by the Government to help track down animal rights extremists behind an escalation of urban terrorism.

In the latest attack a nail-bomb exploded in a North Wales fish and chip shop yesterday.

The owner, Jonathan Davies, 34, a country sports enthusiast, was uninjured when a shower of nails hit the floor of the busy shop in Holywell.

There was a bang like a 12-bore shotgun going off,' his father, Mike, 61, said. 'Luckily he opened the package the wrong way up.'

Concern has been growing in Whitehall for some time about militants' increasingly violent behaviour.

The principal target for the extremists has been Huntingdon Life Sciences, an animal testing laboratory in Cambridgeshire. Last year there were fire bomb attacks on cars outside employees' homes and recently shareholders have been harassed.

Adapted from a report by Philip Johnston in the Daily Telegraph

In groups

Are there any circumstances in which direct action involving damage to property or injury to people in order to make a protest can be justified?

Volunteer work gives you the chance to play an active part in your community. Not only do volunteers help others, they also get a lot of value out of the experience themselves. Volunteers can:

- have the satisfaction of knowing they are doing something positive for their community
- make a valuable contribution to society
- develop skills which will help them in the workplace
- learn a variety of vocational skills, including dealing with difficult situations, problem solving and team building.

In groups

1. In what way do you think the actions of the volunteers (right) was an example of putting belief into action? Do you think it made a difference that these people had a religious belief? Why/why not?

2. Talk about what could be done to improve your local environment and who should take action to bring these improvements about.

Miracle work on deprived estate

by Helen Carter

It seemed an almost herculean task for the volunteers to turn round a deprived council estate in 10 days.

But each day a group of 1,000 Christians have descended on the Valley estate in Swinton, Greater Manchester, and successfully transformed it.

They have removed 280 tonnes of rubbish and constructed a park and dog walking area where once there was only rubble, overgrown weeds, discarded syringes and dog mess.

A community garden has been created and an outdoor amphitheatre will be built for the children. More than 200 gardens have been tidied and rubbish has been removed from boarded-up properties which had become dumping grounds.

The Operation Valley project was organised by Greater Manchester police with the help of the volunteers from the Christian group Message 2000 which was in the city for a 10-day summer youth Christian festival …

Janette Ball, secretary of the residents' association, said that many people living on the estate had initially been sceptical about what could be achieved by the volunteers. 'I thought it was extremely ambitious to do everything in 10 days,' she said. 'A lot of people were very cynical at the start. We have come a long way and a lot of work has been done.'

Clare Danquah, one of the volunteers, said: 'We were putting our faith into action. The first day we were mostly removing rubbish. We found old car engines and sofas which had been dumped. The great thing is that we have been able to see the results pretty instantly.'

From *The Guardian*

Community Service Volunteers

Community Service Volunteers (CSV) is a national organisation dedicated to providing opportunities for everyone to get involved in their local community. CSV offers a wide range of different volunteer opportunities, from befriending house-bound people, to helping people learn to read, to enabling people with disabilities to lead independent lives. Because CSV has strong links with so many organisations throughout the country, it can provide a wide range of volunteer roles to suit a wide range of people.

As well as placing people in suitable work schemes, CSV provides nationally recognised and accredited training courses for volunteers. CSV volunteers can gain valuable vocational skills in sectors as diverse as business administration, childcare, IT, leisure and hairdressing. Training is provided throughout the UK and the only qualifications you need are a willingness and enthusiasm to learn and to volunteer your time.

In groups

Find out more about CSV and its work in your area. Where is your local CSV office? What kind of schemes do they run in your community? Present your findings to the class.

Index

abortion 86–87
achievements 34–35
acne 44
AIDS 54
aggressive behaviour 10
alcohol and drinking 56–59
anger 12–13, 43
animal rights 94
appearance 8, 36–40
arguments 72
arranged marriages 80
AS/A2 and A levels 30–33
assertive behaviour 10–11
AVCEs 30–31, 33
babies 82–85
beliefs 7, 92–95
bereavement 76–77
body language 29
body piercing 45
breaking up 69, 74
BTECs 30–31, 33
budgets 20
bullying 71, 92
cannabis 62
careers 24–29
children 82–85
chlamydia 55
cohabitation 79
commitment 66, 78–81
communication 29, 50, 67, 72
condoms 50, 52
contraception 50–52
CV 28
death 76–77, 90–91
degrees 30–31
depression 48–49
diets 38–39
divorce and separation 74–75, 81
drugs and drugtaking 60–65
eating disorders 36–39
emotions 10–13, 43, 46, 67, 69, 74, 76
employment 30, 32–33
euthanasia 90–91
exams 18–19

exercise 40–41
extroverts 6
families 72–77
fashion 8, 36–37
feelings 67, 68
fogging 11
food 36–39, 43
friends 7, 66–71
further education 30–33
gap year 33
GCSEs 30
genetically modified foods 89
genetic engineering 88
GNVQs 30–31, 33
grief 76–77
harassment 92–93
health 36, 38–39, 40–41, 42–45,
          46–49, 52–55, 56–58, 60, 65
heroes 9
heroin 65
HIV 54–55
homophobia 71
homosexuality 70–71
HNDs 30–31
ideals 9, 36–37
image 6–9, 36–37
independence 23, 72–73
International Baccalaureate 30–31
interviews 29
introverts 6
jealousy 68
job applications 27
jobs 24–29, 32–33
Key Skills 31
lifestyle 6–9, 41
living wills 91
love 66–71, 81
managing time 14–15
marriage 78–81, 85
media 7, 36–37
money 20–23, 32, 84
moral dilemmas 86–91
NVQs 30

on-line credit 21
parenting 82–85
partnerships 66–71, 78–81
passive behaviour 10
periods 42–43
personality 6, 66, 82
personal qualities and skills 24–25
personal statements 34–35
prejudice 70–71, 92–93
pre-menstrual syndrome 42–43
pressure 46–47
qualifications 30–32
racism 92
relationships 66–71, 78–81
responsibility 50, 72, 82–83
revision 16–17
rights 72–73
safer sex 50–55
same-sex relationships 70–71
sex 50–55, 59
sexism 93
sexually transmitted infections
          52–53
skills 25
skin problems 43, 44
social dilemmas 86–91
stress 46–47
study skills 14–19
suicide 49, 77
suntanning 45
tattoos 45
time management 14–15
training 30, 33
values 7
violent protest 94
Vocational A levels 30–31, 33
vocational courses 30
volunteer work 95